Phonics for Middle-Grade Students

BY

MYRL SHIREMAN

COPYRIGHT © 1998 Mark Twain Media, Inc.

ISBN   10-digit: 1-58037-069-1
       13-digit: 978-1-58037-069-1

Printing No. CD-1300

Mark Twain Media, Inc., Publishers
Distributed by Carson-Dellosa Publishing Company, Inc.

Table of Contents

Introduction

All middle-grade students need to be proficient in the use of phonics to recognize unknown words. Phonics is one of the basic word recognition skills that must not be neglected. Unfortunately today, many students reach middle school without having mastered, and in some cases, without having been introduced to phonics and structural analysis. The fact that these students depend almost entirely on a sight vocabulary severely limits their ability to read and interpret middle-school texts and assignments.

The activities in this book are designed for students with various levels of understanding of phonics and structural analysis. Although the activities are developed sequentially, they may be used in any order that fits the specific skill levels of your students.

An important aspect of learning to use phonics and structural analysis is having the opportunity to apply the learned skill. Therefore, most skill activities will include application activities. The application activities require students to both read and write. The reading activities require students to apply recognition of key phonics and structural analysis skills. The writing of sentences requires students to apply the phonics and structural analysis skills correctly in a written context. Students need to understand that it is the context in which a word is used that helps determine the correct pronunciation.

Information "To the Teacher" is included in the front of the book and is keyed to specific activities and sections throughout the book. This information gives instructions and suggestions the teacher may use before assigning activities from the book. It is the teacher's choice whether or not to use the suggested teaching format.

The exercises in this book are mainly designed for middle-school students who have not mastered basic phonics skills. Many middle-school students have these skills and will not benefit from the activities. The teacher must determine the activities that fit the needs of the students. Several activities covering each topic are included to provide those students who need extra practice with the opportunity to do so. Not all students will need to complete every activity. Some may grasp the concept after one or two activities and be ready to move on. The goal of this text is to provide the teacher with resources for those students who need added reinforcement on a topic, while allowing others in the class to move forward at their own pace.

—The Author—

To the Teacher:
Instructions and Suggestions
to Accompany Student Activities

To the Teacher:

When using these exercises with middle-school students who have not mastered basic phonics skills, it will often be necessary to read the directions with the students and offer examples and guided practice until the student understands the concept.

When teaching students to use phonics as a word analysis skill, it is important to note that the pronunciation of many words cannot be determined using phonics. These are words that must be taught as whole words. These are often called **irregular words**.

Examples of irregular words are: beret, acre, tortilla, soiree.

To the Teacher (Use With Consonant Sounds Activities, page 16):

When teaching consonant sounds, it is important to note that many consonants maintain the same basic sound in all words. Other consonant sounds, however, change based on the pattern of letters in a word. The activities that follow begin with consonant sounds that remain constant from word to word.

Have students listen carefully as you pronounce each of the following words. Pronounce the word slowly so that each sound is apparent but not distorted. Have students write the beginning consonant heard as you pronounce each word. The following procedure is suggested for presenting the words.

bat: Say "b-a-t. The boy hit the ball with the b-a-t. b-a-t."

Have students number their papers from 1 to 25. Instruct them to listen for the beginning consonant that will be heard at the beginning of each word. Prepare the students by having them listen carefully as you pronounce the following words. Check to see that students understand what they are expected to do.

bat: Say "b-a-t. The boy hit the ball with the b-a-t. b-a-t."

What letter makes the sound heard at the beginning of "bat"? Have students respond, and then write the letter "b" on the board. Tell the students to listen as you say the word "bat" again and listen for the sound made by the letter "b."

rat: Say "r-a-t. The r-a-t was caught in the trap. r-a-t."

What letter makes the sound heard at the beginning of "rat"? Have students respond, and then write the letter "r" on the board. Tell the students to listen as you say the word "rat" again and listen for the sound made by the letter "r."

Pronounce each of the following words using the procedure described above. Have students write the letter that makes the beginning sound of each word.

1. bus	6. like	11. zero	16. zoo	21. belt
2. date	7. map	12. nickel	17. mother	22. jump
3. fan	8. number	13. pizza	18. judge	23. rose
4. gate	9. rope	14. radio	19. gas	24. paper
5. job	10. visit	15. valley	20. fish	25. nod

To the Teacher (Use Before Rime Activities, page 17):

There are many letter cominations that can be used to make many words by adding a consonant or consonant blend to the letter combination. For example, the letter combination "ale" can form the nucleus of many new words by adding consonants to the "ale" combination (ale, sale, bale, tale, male, pale, and so on).

Letter combinations like "ale" are called **rimes**. The consonant or consonant blend added to the letter combination is called an **onset**.

Teaching students to observe rimes and use onsets can become a very positive word identification skill for middle-grade students. Use the following to introduce students to rimes and onsets.

Students must be able to read the words "ask" and "old." If they cannot, teach these words to students using the following steps.

Teach students to pronounce the word as /a—s—k/. Write the word on the board. Focus the students on your finger or pointer placed under the first letter in the word. Have students listen as you pronounce the word while slowly moving your finger/pointer from left to right beneath the word.

Have students pronounce the words as you move your finger/pointer from left to right. Have the students write the word.

Use the same procedure for "old."

Write the word "__ ask" in column form on the board three times.

    __ ask
    __ ask
    __ ask

Tell the students to watch as you write the letter "t" on the blank in front of "__ ask." Ask: "What word have I made?" Do the same with the letters "b" and "m." Have the class pronounce all three words.

Write the word "old" as "__ old" in column form on the board three times.

    __ old
    __ old
    __ old

Tell the students to watch as you write the letter "t" on the blank in front of "__ old." Ask: "What word have I made?" Do the same with the letters "b" and "m." Have the class pronounce all three words.

To the Teacher (Use With Rime Activities, beginning on page 17):

For the exercises that follow, it is important that students can recognize and pronounce the root words or rimes used. Write the words on the board, and have the class pronounce each word.

To the Teacher (Use With Vowel Sounds Activity 14, page 22):

Write the words **"so," "no," "me," "he," "be,"** and **"go"** on the board and discuss how the words are alike. It is important for the students to determine that the words end in a vowel and the vowel says its name (it is a long vowel sound).

Pronounce each of the words and ask the students to tell how many vowel sounds they hear as the word is pronounced. Students should determine that (1) each word has **one vowel sound**; (2) each vowel sound says its name, so it is the **long vowel sound**; (3) each word is a **one-syllable word** because only one vowel sound is heard, and (4) the syllable is an **open syllable**. When a syllable ends in a vowel, it is an open syllable. Note that the pattern of each word is **CV (consonant/vowel)**.

To the Teacher (Use with Vowel Sounds Activity 15, pages 22–23):

Write the words **"sod," "not," "met," "hen," "bed,"** and **"got"** on the board and discuss how the words are alike. It is important for the students to determine that the words have a vowel between two consonants and that the vowel does not say its name. The vowel sound is the short sound. Each word is a closed syllable because the syllable pattern is consonant/vowel/consonant.

Pronounce each of the words and ask the students to tell how many vowel sounds they hear as the word is pronounced. Students should determine that (1) each word has **one vowel sound**, (2) each vowel sound is the **short vowel sound**, (3) each word is a **one-syllable word** because only one vowel sound is heard, and (4) the syllable is a **closed syllable**. Note that the pattern of each word is **CVC (consonant/vowel/consonant)**.

To the Teacher (Use With Vowel Sounds Activity 16, page 23):

Review the meaning of long and short vowel sounds. Review the symbols placed over the vowel to mark the long and short sounds: macron (‾), breve (˘).

Write the words **"cape," "cute," "cove," "kite,"** and **"hate"** on the board. Have a discussion and help the students determine that (1) there are **two vowels** in each word, (2) each word **ends in the letter "e,"** (3) the sound for **the letter "e" is silent** in each word, (4) there is **one vowel sound heard**, and (5) the **vowel sound is long**. Note that the pattern for each word is **CVCe̸**. Tell the students that the symbol used to mark the silent "e" will be a slash through the "e": "e̸."

Ask the students the number of vowels seen in each word. Then pronounce each word and ask the students the number of vowel sounds heard. Indicate to the students that each word has one syllable, since only one vowel sound is heard when each word is pronounced.

To the Teacher (Use With Vowel Combinations Activities 20–25, pages 27–32):

In preparing students for the following activities, make sure they can pronounce the key words for each activity.

seat	**head**
die	**chief**
either	**eight**
pool	**took**
know	**cow**

To the Teacher (Use Before Initial Blends Activity 26, page 33):

Students need to become familiar with the initial blends **cr, gr, fl, dr, fr, bl, br, cl, pl, pr, sch, sl, sm, sn, sp, spl, spr, squ, st, str, sw, tr,** and **tw**. Students need some practice listening and writing the blends, as words that contain the blends are pronounced. Students need to know that a blend is a combination of consonants. Each consonant can be heard when the blend is part of a word.

Write the blends **cr, gr, fl, dr, fr, bl, br, cl, pl, pr, sch, sl, sm, sn, sp, spl, spr, squ, st, str, sw, tr,** and **tw** on the board. Tell the students these are combinations of consonants that form the beginnings of many words. Remind the students that these combinations are called **blends** because **each of the letters can be heard when the word is pronounced**. Write the words **black, smack, stack,** and **flack** on the board. Have the students listen as you slowly pronounce the words one at a time. After pronouncing each word, ask the students to note the sound of the blend. Have them write the blend. Ask if they know other words that begin with the sound of the blend. Erase the words, but **leave the blends** written on the board and continue with the following.

Have the students take out a piece of paper. Tell them you will pronounce some words. As you pronounce a word, students are to refer to the board and write the blend they hear for each word.

Pronounce each word in the list below. Give a simple sentence using the word. Pronounce the word again. Tell the students to refer to the board and write the blend they hear at the beginning of each word.

blaze	**brat**	**cloud**	**crime**	**drink**	**flat**
friend	**glass**	**grade**	**plant**	**slap**	**school**
snack	**splash**	**spree**	**street**	**prank**	**small**
spook	**squish**	**stop**	**swell**	**trip**	**twist**

To the Teacher (Use Before Final Blends Activity 27, page 34):

Students that can use blends in the initial position are ready for activities that will help them develop skill in using blends that occur in the final position.

Write the blends **ft, nt, nd, ng, nk, pt, st, lk,** and **sp** on the board. Tell the students these are combinations of consonants that are found at the end of many words. Tell the students that these combinations are blends because each of the letters can be heard when the word is pronounced. Write the words **gift, front, band, sang, tank, except, grasp, milk,** and **test** on the board. Have the students listen as you slowly pronounce the words one at a time. After pronouncing each word, ask the students to note the sound of the blend. Have them write the blend. Ask if they know other words that end with the sounds of the blend. Erase the words but leave the blends written on the board and continue with the activity that follows.

Have the students take out a piece of paper. Tell them you will pronounce some words. The students are to refer to the board and write the blend they hear at the end of each word.

Pronounce each word. Give a simple sentence that includes the word. Pronounce the word again. Tell the students to refer to the board and write the blend they hear at the end of each word.

thank	**pound**	**plant**	**raft**	**silk**
fast	**king**	**kept**	**gasp**	**prompt**

To the Teacher (Use With Activity 28, pages 35–36):

For students to complete this activity, they must understand that the number of syllables in a word is determined by the vowel sounds heard when the word is pronounced. A word may have three vowels, but only two vowels may be heard when it is pronounced.

Example: **"note"** has two vowels. However, only one vowel sound is heard when the word is pronounced; therefore, the word has one syllable.

Example: **"prevail"** has three vowels. However, only two vowels sounds are heard when the word is pronounced; therefore, the word has two syllables.

If students need more work to ensure understanding, use the following words. Visually show the word and then pronounce the word. Have students note the number of vowels in the word and the number of vowel sounds heard when the word is pronounced. The number of syllables is determined by the number of vowel sounds heard in a word.

drink (1 syll.)	**exercise (3 syll.)**	**excite (2 syll.)**	**trial (1 syll.)**
diploma (3 syll.)	**boil (1 syll.)**	**perfume (2 syll.)**	**triangle (3 syll.)**

To the Teacher (Use Before Digraph Activity 32, pages 39–40):

Students need to become familiar with initial digraphs. Digraphs are often harder for students than blends. Digraphs are two consonants that stand for a sound that is unlike either of the consonants. The best example to use in explaining the concept to students is the digraph **"ph."** Write the words **"phone"** and **"phrase"** on the board. Pronounce the words slowly while the students listen. Ask them what sound they hear at the beginning of each word. What letter makes that sound?

Write the digraphs **"ch," "th," "ph," "sh,"** and **"gh"** on the board. Tell the students these are combinations of consonants that form the beginning of many words. Tell the students that these combinations are called **digraphs** because the two letters together make a sound unlike either of the two letters.

Refer back to "phone" and "phrase" on the board. Write the letter **"f"** above the **"ph"** in each word. Call attention to the fact that the letters **"ph"** make the sound for **"f,"** which is unlike **"p"** or **"h."**

Write the words **"chin," "ghost," "physical," "sheep,"** and **"than"** on the board. Write the digraphs **"ch," "gh," "ph," "sh,"** and **"th"** on the board. Have the students listen as you slowly pronounce the words one at a time. After pronouncing each word, ask the students to note the sound of the digraph. Have the students refer to the list of digraphs and write the one they hear as you pronounce the words. Ask if they know other words that begin with the sounds of the digraphs listed. Erase the words, but leave the digraphs written on the board and continue with the following.

Have the students take out a piece of paper. Tell them you will pronounce some words. The students are to refer to the board and write the digraph they hear as you pronounce each word. Check the students following each pronounced word to insure that students are correctly recognizing the digraphs pronounced.

Pronounce each word. Give a simple sentence using the word. Pronounce the word again. Tell the students to refer to the board and write the digraph they hear at the beginning of each word.

cheese	**phonics**	**shine**	**this**
chicken	**shield**	**that**	**ghastly**

To the Teacher (Use Before Activity 33, page 41):
Some digraphs require special attention because they produce a different sound in different words. The digraph **"ch"** is a digraph that is pronounced differently in some words. Write the words **"church,"** **"chef,"** and **"school"** on the board. Pronounce the words slowly and ask the students to indicate the sound made by "ch" in each word. Write the letters "ch" above the "ch" in church. Write the letters "sh" above the letters "ch" in chef. Write the letter "k" above the "ch" in school.

Pronounce each of the words in Activity 33 to insure that students can pronounce each word. Have the class chorally pronounce each of the words, and then assign the activity.

To the Teacher (Use Before Activity 35, pages 43–44):
Students that can use digraphs in the initial position are ready for activities that will help them develop skill in using digraphs that occur in the final position.

Write the digraphs **"ph,"** **"ch,"** **"ck,"** **"sh,"** **"gh,"** **"lk,"** and **"th"** on the board. Tell the students these are combinations of letters that are found at the end of many words. Remind the students that these combinations are called digraphs because the combination of consonants makes a new sound not made by either of the consonants themselves.

Write the words **"beach,"** **"clock,"** **"cough,"** **"silk,"** **"crash,"** and **"both"** on the board. Have the students listen as you slowly pronounce the words and underline the digraphs. After pronouncing each word, ask the students to note the sound of the digraph. Have them write the digraph. Ask if they know other words that end with the sound of the digraph. Erase the words, but leave the digraphs written on the board and continue with the following activity.

Have the students take out a piece of paper. Tell them you will pronounce some words. The students are to refer to the board and write the digraph they hear at the end of each word.

Pronounce each word. Give a simple sentence that includes the word. Pronounce the word again. Tell the students to refer to the board and write the digraph they hear at the end of each word.

bunch	**lash**	**health**	**tough**	**bulk**	**shack**

trophy (Tell students that the digraph is in the medial position in this word.)

To the Teacher (Use With Activity 37 pages, 46–47):
Tell the students that words beginning with the letter **"c"** may have a **soft or hard sound**. Pronounce **"cent."** Ask: "What sound do you hear at the beginning?" Point to the letter "c" on the board. Ask: "What is the name of this letter?" "What is the sound of this letter in "cent"?" Make sure that students understand that the name of the letter is "c." However, in the word "cent," the letter "c" makes the **/s/ or soft sound**. Have all of the students say "cent" chorally. Call attention to where the tongue is placed to make the sound of "c" in "cent."

Follow the same procedure with the word **"cabin."** Make sure that students understand that the name of the letter is "c." However, in the word "cabin," the letter "c" makes the **/k/ or hard sound**. Have all of the students say "cabin" chorally. Call attention to how the "c" sound is made in "cabin."

Use the above procedure to present the words **"cucumber"** and **"cinnamon"** to demonstrate the hard and soft sound of "c." Tell the students to listen carefully as you pronounce the two words. Write the words on the board. Pronounce the words slowly while moving your hand from left to right under the word as each part is pronounced. Point to the beginning of each word and have the students rewrite the letter "c" or "k" to indicate the sound heard.

The following words are to be pronounced for the students as they complete Activity 37.

1. coffee	2. cider	3. collie	4. camel	5. century
6. circus	7. cage	8. cement	9. cycle	10. cyclone

To the Teacher (Use With Activity 38, pages 48–49):
The sounds associated with the letter **"g"** are called **the soft or hard sounds of "g."** When "g" sounds like "j," it is called the soft sound of "g." Words like "giant" and "gym" have the soft sound for "g." Present **"giant"** and **"gym"** on the board or overhead to the students. Have students pronounce the words. If students cannot pronounce the words, teach the words to the students.

Pronounce each word slowly. Now have the class pronounce the words slowly two or three times.

Tell the students that words beginning with the letter "g" may have the soft or hard sound of "g." Pronounce "giant." Ask: "What sound do you hear at the beginning?" Point to the letter "g" on the board. "What is the name of this letter?" "What is the sound of this letter in "giant"?" Make sure that students understand that the name of the letter is "g." In the word "giant," the letter "g" makes **the soft sound of "g."** Have all of the students say "giant" chorally. Call attention to where the tongue is placed to make the sound of "g" in "giant."

Follow the same procedure with the word **"gym."**

Now present the word **"gold"** on the board or overhead. In the word "gold," the letter "g" makes **the hard sound of "g."** Have all of the students say "gold" chorally. Call attention to where the tongue is placed to make the sound of "g" in "gold."

Follow the same procedure with the word **"go."**

The following words are to be pronounced for the students as they complete Activity 38.

1. geometry	2. gem	3. girl	4. go	5. gallon
6. gentle	7. giraffe	8. gorilla	9. guitar	10. gyro

To the Teacher (Hard/Soft Sound Spelling Exercises):

The following words have the **soft or hard sound of the letter "c."** These words may be presented as a spelling exercise to reinforce student understanding. Have students write "hard/soft" following each word spelled. Use List A or List B depending on the phonics skills of the students.

List A:

1. cage	2. cinder	3. civil	4. calendar	5. carnival	6. citizen
7. cannon	8. ceremony	9. cyclone	10. capture	11. canteen	12. cement
13. carbon	14. capital	15. catalog			

List B:

1. cat	2. can	3. cider	4. cot	5. cent	6. cell	7. city	8. cake

The following words have the **soft or hard sound of the letter "g."** These words may be presented as a spelling exercise to reinforce student understanding. Have students write "hard/soft" following each word spelled. Use List A or List B depending on the phonics skills of the students.

List A:

1. garage	2. gallon	3. general	4. gallant	5. germ	6. gesture
7. garment	8. gentle	9. globe	10. gather	11. grape	12. geography
13. gypsy	14. ginger	15. grand			

List B:

1. gas	2. gab	3. gem	4. good	5. gyp	6. golf	7. go	8. got

To the Teacher (Use Before Syllabication Activity 50, page 62):

It is important that students understand the concept of a syllable before beginning syllabication activities. Review vowel sounds (long, short, and the schwa) prior to beginning syllabication activities.

Students also need to review that the number of vowel sounds heard, not the number of vowels in the word, determines the number of syllables in a word. Activity 50 on page 62 will help develop the concept that the number of vowel sounds must be determined.

The purpose of the activity is to reinforce the fact that the number of vowel sounds heard determines the number of syllables in a word. Therefore, before beginning the activity, review the pronunciation of the words with the class to make certain that students understand the correct pronunciation of the words.

To the Teacher (Use With Syllibication Activities, page 63, or Before Phonics Review, pages 98–99):
 Indicate to the students that in a polysyllabic word where there are two consonants between two vowels, the syllable division will usually occur between the two consonants, unless the first vowel has a long sound. **VCCV** is the pattern found in words for this rule.

ob/ject	mon/key	per/fect	mis/take	but/ter	cab/bage
lad/der	bal/loon	com/mon	cop/per	skim/ming	

 VCCV words with the first vowel having the long sound, as in **secret** and **microbe** are usually divided after the vowel in the first syllable. In this case students must read the text to determine which syllable division makes sense in the context. If the word doesn't make sense, then reread and apply the other vowel sound.

 Syllables are classified as open or closed. **Open syllables** are those that end with a vowel sound. **Closed syllables** are those that end with a consonant sound.
 Words with open syllables: **secret, ponies, tiger, stories, famous**
 Words with closed syllables: **sunset, monkey, butter, rabbit, circle**

 Indicate to the students that when there is one consonant between two vowels in a polysyllabic word (**VCV pattern**), the consonant **usually** goes with the second vowel if the preceding vowel has a long sound. If the first vowel has a short sound, the consonant stays with the first vowel. If the consonant between the two vowels is either "x" or "y," this letter usually remains with the preceding vowel to form the syllable.
 Write the following words on the board and have students divide the words into syllables.
 VCV words where a consonant begins the second syllable:

fatal	paper	delay	ever	begin	sable
tiger	grocer	total	amuse	police	acorn

 Write the following words on the board and have students divide the words into syllables with the vowel beginning the second syllable. Note that when these words are pronounced using this syllable division, they are common words with which the students are familiar.

shiver	novel	comet	solid	taxi	exert
peril	robin	rapid	travel	money	mimic

 Next have the students divide these same words with the consonant beginning the second syllable. Note that when these words are pronounced, they are not familiar. It is not the correct pronunciation. Make the point that with the VCV pattern, when a word is divided and it does not make sense when it is pronounced, then one should divide the word so the second syllable begins with a vowel.

To the Teacher (Activity 51, page 63):
 Write the ten words used in Activity 51 in a column on the board. Use one of the words and review consonants and vowels quickly. Check to make sure students can pronounce each word. Have students discuss how the words are alike. Continue discussion until students determine that each word has two consonants between two vowels. Then introduce the following rule for dividing the word into syllables. **(Rule: When there are two consonants between two vowels, the syllable division is usually between the two consonants.)** Complete the blanks for the word "butter" with the students to insure understanding of the activity.
 In learning to blend sounds, it is important that students practice blending the syllables in each word. After the students complete the activity, refer to the words written on the board. Have students indicate where the syllable division was made. Have students indicate the vowel sound in each syllable. Blend the sounds for each syllable and pronounce the word chorally.

To the Teacher (Activity 53, page 65):
 Students have learned that when two consonants are between two vowels, the syllable division is between the two consonants. When a digraph appears, it is usually an exception to this rule. Students need to practice syllable division with the exceptions so they realize that the general rule has exceptions.

To the Teacher (Activity 54, page 66):

Write the ten words used in Activity 54 in a column on the board. Use one of the words and review vowel sounds (long, short, schwa). Check to make sure students can pronounce each word. Have students discuss how the words are alike. Continue discussion until students identify the spelling pattern is **VCV**. Then introduce the rule for dividing the word into syllables. **(Rule: When a consonant is between two vowels, the syllable division is usually before the consonant.)**

In learning to blend sounds, it is important that students practice blending the syllables in each word. Refer to the words from Activity 54 written on the board, and have students indicate where the syllable division should be made. Have students indicate the vowel sound in each syllable. Blend the sounds for each syllable and pronounce the word chorally. Complete the blanks for the word "open" with the students to insure understanding of the activity.

To the Teacher (Activity 56, page 68):

Write the ten words used in Activity 56 in a column on the board. Use one of the words and review vowel sounds (long, short, schwa). Check to make sure students can pronounce each word. Have students discuss how the words are alike. Continue discussion until students determine that each word **ends in a consonant followed by the letters "le."** Then introduce the rule for dividing the word into syllables. **(Rule: When a word ends in "le" with a consonant before the "l," the pattern is "consonant le" or "Cle". The combination "Cle" forms a syllable.)** Complete the blanks for the word "simple" with the students to insure understanding of the activity.

In learning to blend sounds, it is important that students practice blending the syllables in each word. This group of words offers an excellent opportunity to reinforce the students' understanding of the **schwa** sound. Refer to the list of words from Activity 56 on the board, and have students indicate where the syllable division should be made. Have students indicate the vowel sound in each syllable. Blend the sounds for each syllable and pronounce the word chorally. During blending, call attention to the schwa sound that occurs in the final syllable. The schwa sound is similar to the short sound of the vowel "u."

To the Teacher (Use With Structural Analysis Activity 58, page 70):

Structural analysis activities can be very effective in improving the reading, writing, and spelling skills of middle-school students. The structural analysis activities that follow will include **compound words, prefixes, roots,** and **suffixes**. To understand structural analysis, students must first understand roots. Suffixes and prefixes are additions to the back and front of the root and are known as **affixes**. Suffixes will be presented before prefixes. **Suffixes may be inflectional or derivational.** Inflectional suffixes are much easier for students to understand, and the activities are appropriate for many middle-school students. Derivational suffixes are more difficult since the suffix often changes the part of speech of the word to which the suffix is added. The suffix activities included in the book will emphasize both inflectional and derivational suffixes.

There are a few suffixes and prefixes that have great utility in reading at the middle-school level. Therefore, the activities will emphasize selected suffixes and prefixes.

Introduce students to the concept of root words by writing the following words on the board or overhead. Underline "play" in each of the words. Tell the students that the root word in the group is the word "play." Point out that **"re," "ing,"** and **"ed"** are examples of affixes (parts added to the root word), which they will learn about in the activities that follow.

> **play**   **replay**   **playing**   **replayed**

Write the words **obey, disobey,** and **disobeying** on the board. Have the students write the root word in each of these words. Check the students to make sure they understand and are correctly completing the assignment. Then have them write the affixes.

Write the following words on the board and have the students write the root word and the affixes.

> **overpay**   **underpay**   **pay**   **underpayment**   **underpayed**

Call attention to the fact that the root of each of the words above is a **root word**. Let the students discuss how the root has changed. Have them suggest definitions of a root word. For example: A basic word to which other word parts (affixes) known as suffixes and prefixes have been added.

To the Teacher (Use With Compound Word Activities, beginning on page 89):
Compound words are formed when two complete words combine to create a new word. Some compound words have basically the same meaning as that expressed by the two words that combined to form the compound. However, many compound words have a meaning that is different from the meaning of the words making the compound.

Some compound words are formed from two words to form a new word with a meaning *somewhat* different from the two forming the compound.

Example: **basketball**

Some compound words are formed from two words to form a new word with a meaning that is *much different* from the words that form the compound word.

Examples: **butterfly   fireworks   hardware   peppermint**

For syllabication purposes, when a word is composed of two complete words to make a compound word, the word is divided between the two words.

Examples: **some/where   bird/house   cow/boy**

Tell the students that a compound word is a combination of two words. Use the examples below to make certain that students understand the concept of compound words. Write the words on the board or overhead and call attention to the two words that combine to form the compound word. Separate the compound word and underline the two words that make the compound word.

football   foot ball   doorbell   door bell

Write the following words on the board or overhead and ask the students to find the words that combine to make the compound words.

somewhere   anyplace

To the Teacher (Use Before Accent Activities, page 92):
Students need practice in identifying the accented syllable and in applying accent to syllables in context. It is context that helps the student understand that the first pronunciation of a word my not make sense in all cases.

Practice the following with the students to prepare them for activities on accented and unaccented syllables. Write **"re'cord"** and **"re cord'"** on the board. Call attention to the (') mark. Tell the students that this mark tells which syllable is accented or sounded harder when a word is pronounced. Have them listen as you read the following sentences and tell which syllable is stressed or sounded harder.

1. The **record** player was no longer needed. (re cord')
2. When the game is over, **record** the winner. (re'cord)
3. His **object** was to win the race. (ob'ject)
4. He didn't **object** to the decision. (ob ject')

Name _____ Date _____

Learning to Use the Dictionary

ACTIVITY 1 ALPHABETIZING

One of the important skills in using the dictionary is the ability to locate words. The words in the dictionary are arranged **alphabetically**.

Alphabetize the following vocabulary words. Place the first word alphabetically on line 1, the second on line 2, and so on. Complete Group One and check your work. Then, complete Group Two.

Group One		Group Two	
giant	1._____	germ	1._____
magic	2._____	stage	2._____
nudge	3._____	agent	3._____
ago	4._____	magic	4._____
vegetable	5._____	good	5._____
orange	6._____	range	6._____
red	7._____	code	7._____
wager	8._____	algebra	8._____
table	9._____	grit	9._____
flood	10._____	aghast	10._____
vertical	11._____	orange	11._____
boon	12._____	original	12._____
range	13._____	algae	13._____
creed	14._____	gutter	14._____
peach	15._____	magnet	15._____
jelly	16._____	stale	16._____
sale	17._____	dorsal	17._____
king	18._____	color	18._____
deed	19._____	grill	19._____
dead	20._____	stake	20._____
fan	21._____	juice	21._____
heavy	22._____	stole	22._____
land	23._____	found	23._____
punt	24._____	number	24._____
yellow	25._____	quart	25._____

10

Name _____ Date _____

ACTIVITY 2 GUIDE WORDS

On each page of a dictionary you will find the guide words. **Guide words** tell you the first word on the page and the last word on the page. The words on that page are then arranged alphabetically between the guide words. Guide words may be found listed at the top of the page on the left and right sides, or in some dictionaries, the guide words are listed at the top and bottom of the page.

Example 1:   Example 2:
Left side of page   Right side of page   Left top of page   **cooler**
   cooler   **core**   Bottom right of page   **core**

Assume that the guide words for this page are **cooler** and **core**. Select the words from the following list that would appear as entry words on the page with the guide words **cooler** and **core**. Write the words you select on the blank below the list of words.

camera	cord	cordial	cork	corral	copy
cope	copper	coronary	coral	cooper	copra
correct	dandy	curl			

1. _____

_____

Assume that the following list is part of a page found in a dictionary. Answer the questions below.

rectify   **reform**

rectify   reduce
recur   reed
red   reflect
redeemer   reflex
redouble   reform

2. The guide words are _____ and _____ .

3. The entry words are _____

_____ .

Name _____ Date _____

ACTIVITY 3 DICTIONARY PRACTICE

Find the words below in a dictionary and complete the following: (a) Place the phonetic pronunciation in the parentheses. (b) Read the sentence following each word. Use a dictionary to select the meaning that the word has in the sentence. Write the definition you choose on the blank below the sentence. (c) Identify the part of speech of each word as it is used in the sentence.

1a. rectify (_____)   You must **rectify** the mistake you have made.
   b. meaning: _____
   c. part of speech: _____

2a. literate (_____)   The entire class is **literate**.
   b. meaning: _____
   c. part of speech: _____

3a. recur (_____)   Do you think the injury will **recur**?
   b. meaning: _____
   c. part of speech: _____

4a. recall (_____)   The vote was to **recall** the senator.
   b. meaning: _____
   c. part of speech: _____

5a. receipt (_____)   The **receipt** for the shirt was missing.
   b. meaning: _____
   c. part of speech: _____

6a. inwardly (_____)   She kept her thoughts directed **inwardly**.
   b. meaning: _____
   c. part of speech: _____

7a. string (_____)   This win brings the **string** of victories to ten in a row.
   b. meaning: _____
   c. part of speech: _____

8a. honor (_____)   The **honor** was given to him for his long service.
   b. meaning: _____
   c. part of speech: _____

Name _____ Date _____

ACTIVITY 4 THE PRONUNCIATION KEY

In learning to use a dictionary, the pronunciation key is very important. Each dictionary has a different pronunciation key. You must refer to the key in the dictionary when using the dictionary to determine the correct way to pronounce a word.

Use a dictionary of your choice or one assigned by your teacher to write the phonetic pronunciations found in the dictionary for the words below. Write the phonetic pronunciation in the parentheses. Then, on the blanks that follow the parentheses, write the symbols and key words found in the pronunciation key used in the dictionary that would be used to correctly pronounce each of the words.

Title of dictionary: _____

1. banquet (_____) _____

_____

2. govern (_____) _____

_____

3. legislature (_____) _____

_____

4. spiritual (_____) _____

_____

5. supreme (_____) _____

_____

6. checkbook (_____) _____

_____

7. discuss (_____) _____

_____

8. crown (_____) _____

_____

9. phone (_____) _____

_____

10. knife (_____) _____

_____

Name _____ Date _____

ACTIVITY 5 PRONUNCIATION SYMBOLS

Each word in Column A is the dictionary pronunciation of a word. Write the actual word on the blank in Column B. Use the following symbols to help determine the word.

macron long vowel symbol (ˉ)	breve short vowel symbol (˘)	schwa (ə)

Column A	Column B
1. fēt	_____
2. fĕs′tə vəl	_____
3. mīn	_____
4. bŭt′'n	_____
5. kā′bəl	_____
6. hāst	_____
7. ē′kwəl	_____
8. dē sīd′	_____
9. rē′sĕs	_____
10. myōot′'n ē	_____
11. däl′ər	_____
12. kĕm′ĭ kəl	_____
13. kən fĕs′	_____
14. näm′ə nāt′	_____
15. păsh′ə nĭt	_____
16. wäl′əp	_____
17. tĕks′tĭl′	_____
18. kăn′dē	_____
19. băs′kĭt	_____
20. rī′ət	_____

Name _____ Date _____

ACTIVITY 6 IDENTIFYING PHONETIC SPELLING

In the selection below, the phonetic spellings for certain words are included in parentheses. Read the selection silently. Then read the selection a second time, and on each blank, write the word from the list below the selection that matches the phonetic spelling in the selection.

She saw the (sfîr) 1._____ (ärk′ ĭng′) 2._____ toward her. She (nōō) 3._____that she must (klîr) 4._____ the (sfîr) 5._____ from the (dē fĕn′sĭv) 6._____ end of the (fēld) 7._____. Racing to meet the (sfîr) 8. _____ at just the (ăp′ər tōōn′) 9. _____ time, she (glănsd) 10._____ at the (ə pō′nənt), 11._____ who was hoping to beat her to the point where the (sfîr) 12._____ completed its (ärk) 13._____. She (nōō) 14._____ the (ə pō′nənt) 15._____ would try to (ĭm′păkt′) 16. _____ the (sfîr) 17._____ so that it would fall beneath the (krôs′bär′) 18. _____ and between the posts to (skôr) 19._____ a (point) 20._____ .

Reaching the sphere just before the opponent, she (thrŭst) 21. _____ her foot forward with full (fôrs) 22._____ and felt (ē lāt′ĭd) 23. _____ as she (prō jĕkt′ĭd) 24._____ it in a (par′ə bäl′ik) 25._____ (ärk) 26._____ deep into the opponents' (tĕr′ə tôr′ē) 27. _____. Just as her (fōōt) 28. _____ made contact, she prepared for the (ĭm ə nĕnt) 29._____ (kə lĭzh′ĕn) 30._____ that she would (ĭn kŭr′) 31. _____ with her opponent and shortly found herself (prōn) 32. _____ on the (ground) 33._____ .

Rising from the ground, she (ĕn gājd′) 34. _____ in a (tĕt′ à tĕt′) 35. _____ with her (dē jĕk′tĭd) 36. _____ (ăd′vər sĕr′ē) 37. _____ as her (tēm) 38. _____ scored the (krōō′shəl) 39. _____ (gōl) 40. _____ .

WORD LIST

parabolic	collision	imminent	thrust	prone	adversary
sphere	arcing	projected	goal	knew	clear
defensive	territory	tête-à-tête	opponent	ground	glanced
opportune	arc	crossbar	score	point	engaged
dejected	elated	field	impact	incur	team
force	crucial				

Name _____ Date _____

Learning About Consonant Sounds

ACTIVITY 7 **INITIAL AND FINAL CONSONANT SOUNDS**

In the list below, there are words that begin with the same consonant sounds. Place all of the words that begin with the same sound on the blanks below the letter that makes that sound.

tack	robin	till	nine	bird	down	fail
jump	last	must	test	box	disk	dull
lemon	milk	not	needle	rabbit	roar	listen
match	bus	dust	puff	ladder	fox	nap

b	f	j	l	m
____	____	____	____	____
____	____	____	____	____
____	____	____	____	____
____	____	____	____	____

n	r	t	d	p
____	____	____	____	____
____	____	____	____	____
____	____	____	____	____

In the list below are words that end with the same sounds. Place all of the words that end with the same sound below the letter that makes that sound.

tack	robin	till	nail	bird	down	buzz
jump	last	car	slam	bed	disk	dull
lemon	milk	nod	need	rabbit	mass	mat
bus	dust	puff	ladder	fuzz	nap	mop

d	f	k	l	m	n
____	____	____	____	____	____
____	____	____	____	____	____
____	____	____	____	____	____
____	____	____	____	____	____

p	r	s	t	z
____	____	____	____	____
____	____	____	____	____
____	____	____	____	____
____	____	____	____	____

Name _____ Date _____

| ACTIVITY 8 | CREATING WORDS WITH CONSONANTS AND RIMES |

In the exercise below the terms "o," "ake," "oy," and "ope" are called **rimes**. You can make many words by adding a letter or letters to the front of a rime.

Place the letters "t," "s," and "n" to make three new words from the rime "o."

1. go   2. ___ o   3. ___ o   4. ___ o

Place the letters "r," "t," "f," "l," and "b" on the blanks to make five new words from the rime "ake."

5. make   6. ___ ake   7. ___ ake   8. ___ ake   9. ___ ake   10. ___ ake

Place the letters "c," "t," and "s" on the blanks to make three new words from the rime "oy."

11. boy   12. ___ oy   13. ___ oy   14. ___ oy

Place the letters "l," "m," "r," "d," and "c" on the blanks to make five new words from the rime "ope."

15. hope   16. ___ ope   17. ___ ope   18. ___ ope   19. ___ ope   20. ___ ope

| ACTIVITY 9 | CREATING WORDS WITH CONSONANTS AND RIMES |

Place one of the letters "f," "p," "c," "m," and "l" on the blanks in 1 through 5 below to make five different words. Then use the words you have made to complete the activity that follows.

1. ___ ast   2. ___ ast   3. ___ ast   4. ___ ast   5. ___ ast

For each of the following sentences, fill in the blanks with the appropriate word from above. Then say the word and write the complete word on the blank at the end of the sentence.

6. He won the race because he is very _ _ _ _ . _____

7. While fishing, he decided to _ _ _ _ the lure near the old stump. _____

8. The ship needed a _ _ _ _ for the sails. _____

9. He was unhappy because he finished _ _ _ _ in the race. _____

10. The _ _ _ _ is history. _____

Match each of the words on the right with its definition on the left.

_____ 11. An important part of a sailing ship   A. last

_____ 12. Describes a runner who wins first place   B. past

_____ 13. The end person in a line   C. mast

_____ 14. What happened yesterday   D. cast

_____ 15. What a fisherman does   E. fast

Name _____ Date _____

ACTIVITY 10 CREATING WORDS WITH CONSONANTS AND RIMES

Place the letters "b," "m," "f," "j," and "w" on the blanks to make five new words.

1.__ ade   2.__ ade   3.__ ade   4.__ ade   5.__ ade

Place the letter blends "bl," "gr," and "sh" on the blanks to make three new words.

6.____ ade   7.____ ade   8.____ ade

Place the letters "t," "l," "m," "p," "r," and "s" on the blanks to make six new words.

9.__ ack   10.__ ack   11.__ ack   12.__ ack   13.__ ack   14.__ ack

Place the letters "arc," "block," "ev," "par," and "tir" on the blanks to make five new words. Write a sentence correctly using each of the words you have made.

15._____ ade

16._____

17._____ ade

18._____

19._____ ade

20._____

21._____ ade

22._____

23._____ ade

24._____

Place the letters "b," "pr," "div," "reb," "surr," and "ref" on the correct blanks to make six new words. Write a sentence correctly using each of the words you have made.

25._____ ound

26._____

27._____ ound

28._____

29._____ ound

30._____

31._____ ide

32._____

33._____ ide

34._____

35._____ orm

36._____

Name _____ Date _____

ACTIVITY 11 CREATING WORDS WITH CONSONANTS AND RIMES

Place the letter "h" on the blank in each of the following. Say the word aloud. Write the word on the second blank, and say the word as you write it.

1. mas__, _____   2. cas__, _____   3. las __, _____

Place the letter "i" on the blank in each of the following. Say the word aloud. Write the word on the second blank, and say the word as you write it.

4. l__st, _____   5. f__st, _____   6. m__st, _____

Read the following selection, silently saying "blank" when a blank occurs. Then reread the selection and write the appropriate word from the list below in the blanks.

last	**past**	**mast**	**fast**	**cast**
cash	**list**	**fist**	**mist**	

When the (7)_____ fisherman was on board, the boat pulled away (8)_____. In the (9)_____ , the (10)_____ of the ship looked like a huge spike. One of the fishermen on the boat (11)_____ his line (12)_____ the bow. A perfect cast! He raised his clenched (13)_____ . The captain checked the (14)_____ and then made sure he had enough (15)_____ to buy the needed supplies.

In Column A is a word. When that word occurs in the list in Column B, circle it.

Column A   **Column B**

16. last   past last mast last last lash list fist last mist last last

17. mast   mast past mast last lash mist mast mast lash cash mast

18. cash   last cash cash mist cast lash last mast cash cash fist

19. fist   fist fist cast fist cast lash fist mast last cash fist fist

20. mist   fist mist fist mist lash cash last mist mist fist fist fist mist

21. cast   cast cast cash cast cash cast cast lash fist mist last

22. lash   lash last lash mist cash last lash lash mist last lash

Name _____ Date _____

ACTIVITY 12 USING RIMES IN SENTENCES

Write the letters of the word that completes each of the following sentences on the blanks in the sentence. Then say the word and write the whole word on the blank following the sentence. Choose from these words:

lack   sack   rack   Mack   pack   back   tack

1. _ _ _ _ was the first one in line. _____
2. He needed help getting the _ _ _ _ on his _ _ _ _ . _____ _____
3. The _ _ _ _ of beans was very heavy. _____
4. He needed a _ _ _ _ and hammer to hang the poster. _____
5. Good players do not _ _ _ _ the desire to play. _____
6. He told Mack to place the balls in the _ _ _ _ on the wall. _____

Complete the statement in Column A with a word from Column B.

Column A
_____ 7. The opposite of front
_____ 8. Put the groceries in the _____.
_____ 9. Hikers wear a _____.
_____ 10. The fishing rods are on the _____.
_____ 11. His name is _____.

Column B
A. pack
B. Mack
C. back
D. sack
E. rack

Read the following selection. When you come to a blank, say "blank." Then read the selection again and place one of the words listed below in each blank.

rack   sack   pack   back

Jack went to the store to buy a (12) _ _ _ _ . He saw a black pack on the (13) _ _ _ _ . Mack helped him get the pack on his (14) _ _ _ _ . The new pack was put in a (15) _ _ _ _ when he left the store.

Read the word in Column A. Then find and circle that same word in Column B.

Column A   **Column B**
16. pack   pack rack tack back pack pack lack pack
17. rack   pack tack rack rack lack back rack tack
18. lack   pack lack lack rack pack tack lack rack
19. back   pack lack back back back back rack tack
20. sack   sack sack back sack rack pack sack lack

Name _____ Date _____

Learning About Consonant Blends

ACTIVITY 26 INITIAL BLENDS

Complete each of the following blanks with one of the blends listed below to create five new words from "ink."

bl	shr	sl	cl	dr

1. _____ ink   2. _____ ink   3. _____ ink   4. _____ ink   5. _____ ink

Each of the words below has one of the blends that is written on the board. Circle the blend in each word. Then write a sentence using the word correctly.

6. stumble _____

7. squad _____

8. school _____

9. scream _____

10. slugger _____

11. promise _____

12. plate _____

13. driver _____

14. great _____

15. brake _____

16. swing _____

17. class _____

18. tromp _____

19. splash _____

20. free _____

Name _____ Date _____

ACTIVITY 27 BLENDS IN THE FINAL POSITION

Each of the words below has one of the blends that is written on the board. Circle the blend in each word. Then write a sentence using the word correctly.

1. soft _____

2. command _____

3. quaint _____

4. thrift _____

5. guest _____

6. crisp _____

7. prong _____

8. corrupt _____

9. shank _____

10. ping _____

11. bend _____

12. cast _____

13. rasp _____

14. plant _____

15. wept _____

16. folk _____

17. craft _____

18. rank _____

19. sing _____

20. went _____

Name _____ Date _____

ACTIVITY 28 CREATING WORDS WITH CONSONANT BLENDS

Complete each of the following blanks with one of the blends below to make a new word. Write a complete sentence using each of the words you have made, and answer the questions that follow after writing the sentences.

ng

1a. fli_____   b. sa_____   c. stu _____   d. so _____

e. _____

f. _____

g. _____

h. _____

i. The vowels in the words above are the letters ___, ___, ___, and ___.

j. The vowel sounds are all (long/short).

k. Each word has how many vowels? _____

l. How many vowel sounds are heard in each word? _____

m. Each of the words has (one/two/three) syllables.

n. Each of the words has a (closed/open) syllable.

pt

2a. ke _____   b. cre _____   c. sle _____   d. prom _____

e. _____

f. _____

g. _____

h. _____

i. The vowels in the words above are the letters ___, ___, ___, and ___.

j. The vowel sounds are all (long/short).

k. Each word has how many vowels? _____

l. How many vowel sounds are heard in each word? _____

m. Each of the words has (one/two/three) syllables.

n. Each of the words has a (closed/open) syllable.

nk

3a. ta _____   b. spa _____   c. bli _____   d. dru _____

e. _____

f. _____

g. _____

Name _____ Date _____

ACTIVITY 28 CREATING WORDS WITH CONSONANT BLENDS (CONT.)

h. _____

i. The vowels in the words above are the letters ____, ____, ____, and ____.

j. The vowel sounds are all (long/short).

k. Each word has how many vowels? _____

l. How many vowel sounds are heard in each word? _____

m. Each of the words has (one/two/three) syllables.

n. Each of the words has a (closed/open) syllable.

nd

4a. spe _____   b. ba _____   c. po _____   d. le _____

e. _____

f. _____

g. _____

h. _____

i. The vowels pronounced in the words above are the letters ____, ____, ____, and ____.

j. The vowel sounds are all (long/short).

k. Each word has how many vowels? _____

l. How many vowel sounds are heard in each word? _____

m. Each of the words has (one/two/three) syllables.

n. Each of the words has a (closed/open) syllable.

ft

5a. le _____   b. dri _____   c. cra _____   d. de _____

e. _____

f. _____

g. _____

h. _____

i. The vowels in the words above are the letters ____, ____, ____, and ____.

j. The vowel sounds are all (long/short).

k. Each word has how many vowels? _____

l. How many vowel sounds are heard in each word? _____

m. Each of the words has (one/two/three) syllables.

n. Each of the words has a (closed/open) syllable.

Name _____ Date _____

ACTIVITY 29   IDENTIFYING AND USING CONSONANT BLENDS

Read the following selection silently. Then circle all of the words that have a blend at the beginning of the word. Write the circled words on the lines below the selection.

Climate is important in determining the animals and plants that grow on the prairie. Some plants are scrawny flowers, while others develop splendid fruit. Some animals and plants struggle in a stressful climate. Some animals, like the grouse, strut with a flourish in a climate that is stressful for others. Others, like the dromedary, plod along like a frigate under the glare of the driver. A blizzard would be a cruel experience for a flamingo. However, to the polar bear, a blizzard may be a gratifying experience faced with bliss.

_____

_____

_____

_____

_____

ACTIVITY 30   IDENTIFYING AND USING CONSONANT BLENDS

Read the following selection. Complete each blank with one of the following blends. Use the blends to make words that make the selection meaningful.

sch	pl	pr	br	sh	sl	sm	spr	gr	str	dr	st	bl
scr	tr	br	cr	sw	cl	spl	tr					

Slowly he opend the (1)_____ ochure and looked at the (2)____ ab picture. His gaze (3)_____ opped on the old wooden (4)____ eachers in the picture. He (5)_____ iled at the thought of the coming season. Since last season, he had looked forward with (6)____ easure to meeting his teammates and participating in the first (7)_____ immage. If the weather was hot, he hoped the coach would remember to have plenty of water to (8)____ ake the team's thirst. He remembered (9)____ ior practices when the team (10)_____ eltered in the high temperatures.

He lay the brochure down and reread the letter the (11)_____ incipal had mailed. The (12)_____ edule for the new season showed that the season would (13)_____ imax with a game against a very (14)_____ ong team. The letter from the principal indicated that a (15)_____ olarship would be very important for those who intended to go on to college after (16)_____ aduating.

Name _____ Date _____

      He thought back to last season when he (17)_____ained his ankle. The sprain forced him to wear a (18)____ int for most of the season. Coach had said a (19)___ acture might not have been as serious as the sprain. It had been a real (20)_____ uggle to (21)_____ amp along the sidelines and watch the team (22)_____ounce the opponents.

      Just then, his (23)_____ other entered the room eating (24)_____occoli. He was wearing a crimson colored (25)_____eat shirt. His brother had come to get his (26)_____ombone to (27)_____actice. He nodded at his brother and (28)_____ rugged when asked if he minded if his brother (29)_____ owsed through the brochure.

ACTIVITY 31   IDENTIFYING AND USING CONSONANT BLENDS

      You have learned that blends are two or three consonants with sounds blended together. You have found that blends may occur at the beginning or at the end of a word. It is also common for blends to occur in the middle of words.

      Each of the words below has a consonant blend in the middle of the word. Find the blend, and write it on the blank following each word.

1. declare _____	2. intrude _____	3. emblem _____
4. inspire _____	5. besmear _____	6. decrease _____
7. enslave _____	8. complex _____	9. unscrew _____
10. bequeath _____	11. comply _____	12. pumped _____
13. selfish _____	14. risky _____	15. paragraph _____

16. After completing these exercises, I know that blends may be at the beginning, at the _____ , or in the _____ of a word.

      Indicate if each of the following is true or false. If a statement is false, correct it on the blank below the statement.

_____ 17. In blends, the sounds of all of the consonants are heard.

_____

_____ 18. Blends are found only at the beginning of a word.

_____

_____ 19. Blends always consist of two consonants.

_____

_____ 20. Blends that are found at the end of a word cannot be used at the beginning of a word.

_____

Name _____ Date _____

Learning About Digraphs

| ACTIVITY 32 | USING DIGRAPHS TO CREATE WORDS |

Complete each of the following blanks with the digraphs listed to make new words. On the blanks following a) and b), add the digraph on the blank to make a new word. On the blank following c), make a new word of your choice using the digraph. Below each word you make, write a sentence using the word you have made.

1. ch

a)_____ in

_____

b) _____ air

_____

c) _____

_____

2. sh

a)_____ in

_____

b) _____ arp

_____

c) _____

_____

3. ph

a)_____ ase

_____

b) _____ ony

_____

c) _____

_____

4. th

a)_____ eir

_____

Name _____ Date _____

ACTIVITY 32 USING DIGRAPHS TO CREATE WORDS (CONTINUED)

b) _____ en

_____

c) _____

_____

5. **wh**

a) _____ at

_____

b) _____ ale

_____

c) _____

_____

Each of the words below contains a digraph. Circle the digraph in each word. Then write a sentence using the word.

6. check _____

7. thunder _____

8. whisper _____

9. whisker _____

10. chief _____

11. ghetto _____

12. thought _____

13. shiver _____

14. phantom _____

15. phrase _____

16. those _____

17. ghoul _____

18. shade _____

19. charge _____

20. whim _____

Name _____ Date _____

ACTIVITY 33 DIGRAPHS THAT MAKE DIFFERENT SOUNDS: "ch"

You have learned that the digraph "ch" can make the sound of "ch" in "church," "sh" in "chef," and "k" in "school." On your own paper, write the words "church," "chef," and "school" in column form as shown below.

/ch/	/sh/	/k/
church	chef	school

Pronounce each of the words below. Write the words that have the "ch" sound in "church" in the column below "church." Write the words that have the "ch" sound in "chef" below "chef." Write the words with the "ch" sound in "school" below "school."

**change   cheek   choke   chivalry   champagne   choose
chandelier   character   choral   chart   chorus**

On the blanks below, write the word "church," "chef," or "school" next to each word to indicate the sound of the "ch" in each word. Then write a sentence correctly using each of the words.

1. change: _____

_____

2. cheek: _____

_____

3. choke: _____

_____

4. chivalry: _____

_____

5. champagne: _____

_____

6. choose: _____

_____

7. chandelier: _____

_____

8. character: _____

_____

9. choral: _____

_____

10. chart: _____

_____

11. chorus: _____

_____

Name _____ Date _____

ACTIVITY 34 IDENTIFYING DIGRAPHS

Read the following selection silently. Then circle all of the words that have a digraph at the beginning of the word. Write the digraphs on the lines below the selection.

Chenille's mother has sent her to the pharmacy to get something for her cough. While walking to the pharmacy, she met some members of her choral group from school. They were going to the theater and then to the church to pick up some photographs. One of her friends wanted to stop at the mall and buy a shirt. The mall was near the wharf, where many spectators came to watch the whales.

After the friend had selected a shirt, she said she was hungry and suggested they go to a restaurant that had a new chef from a foreign land. The friend said the restaurant was sharp because it was built to look like a chalet. When they started, they found that it was necessary to pool their money to pay the bill. After paying the check, each of them had only a small amount of change, but they agreed that the shake and whopper were excellent.

_____

_____

_____

_____

_____

_____

_____

_____

Name _____ Date _____

ACTIVITY 35 DIGRAPHS IN THE FINAL POSITION

Each of the blanks below is followed by a digraph. Write one of the groups of letters in bold on the blanks by each digraph to make a word. Then write a complete sentence using each of the words you have made.

dispat   **grou**   **hat**   **bat**

1a) _____ ch: _____

b) _____ ch: _____

c) _____ ch: _____

d) _____ ch: _____

sma   **fro**   **bri**   **sla**

2a) _____ ck: _____

b) _____ ck: _____

c) _____ ck: _____

d) _____ ck: _____

ba   **smoo**   **clo**   **smi**

3a) _____ th: _____

b) _____ th: _____

c) _____ th: _____

d) _____ th: _____

ra   **sma**   **squi**   **thre**

4a) _____ sh: _____

b) _____ sh: _____

c) _____ sh: _____

d) _____ sh: _____

lau   **cou**   **tou**   **slou**

5a) _____ gh: _____

b) _____ gh: _____

c) _____ gh: _____

d) _____ gh: _____

Name _____ Date _____

ACTIVITY 35 **DIGRAPHS IN THE FINAL POSITION (CONTINUED)**

---

	swi	**fli**	**so**	**cla**

6a) _____ ng: _____

  b) _____ ng: _____

  c) _____ ng: _____

  d) _____ ng: _____

The letter combination "dge" is a special digraph. The three letters combine to form the **soft "g" sound** as in the word "gym." Use the letter combinations below to make five words ending in "dge." On the line beside each word, write a sentence correctly using that word.

	do	**gru**	**smu**	**le**

7a) _____ dge: _____

  b) _____ dge: _____

  c) _____ dge: _____

  d) _____ dge: _____

Each of the words below has a digraph. Write the digraph on the blank. On the line below each blank, write a sentence using the word.

8. fish _____

_____

9. enough _____

_____

10. scratch _____

_____

11. teeth _____

_____

12. rang _____

_____

13. rough _____

_____

14. bridge _____

_____

15. track _____

_____

Name _____ Date _____

ACTIVITY 36 **REVIEWING DIGRAPHS AND BLENDS**

Each of the words below has a digraph. Find the digraph and write it on the blank following each word.

1a) abash ____ b) speck ____ c) rough ____ d) flinch ____

 e) orphan ____ f) gopher ____ g) dolphin ____ h) chamber ____

 i) know ____ j) phase ____ k) beneath ____ l) thousand ____

 m) clack ____

2. After completing the previous exercises, I know that digraphs may be found at the beginning, at the _____ , or in the _____ of a word.

Indicate if each of the following is true or false. If a statement is false, correct it on the blank below each statement.

_____ 3. In digraphs, the sounds of all of the consonants are heard.

_____

_____ 4. Digraphs are found only at the beginning of a word.

_____

Choose a word that you know that fits each of the following descriptions. Then write a sentence using the word. Underline the word you have chosen.

5. A one-syllable word with the short "i" sound. It begins with the "cl" blend and ends with "nk." It is the sound made when two glasses are touched together.

_____

6. A one-syllable word with the short "e" vowel sound and ending in "dge."

_____

7. A two-syllable word with the short "a" vowel sound and ending in "ch." To remove or disconnect.

_____

8. A two-syllable word with the long "a" vowel sound and ending with "ble."

_____

9. A one-syllable word beginning with "th" like in "then." It has a short "a" vowel sound.

_____

10. A one-syllable word beginning with "th" like in "thin." It has a short "a" vowel sound.

_____

Name _____ Date _____

Learning About the Different Sounds Consonants Can Make

| ACTIVITY 37 | THE SOFT AND HARD SOUNDS OF "c" |

You have learned that the letter "c" makes the soft or hard sound when it begins a word. When "c" sounds like "s" in "cent," it is called the soft sound of "c." When "c" sounds like "k," it is called the hard sound of "c."

For the following activity, your teacher will pronounce some words that begin with the letter "c." The sound heard at the beginning of some words will be "s," and for others it will be "k." After a word is pronounced, write the letter "s" or "k" below to show the sound you hear at the beginning of each word. Then write "soft" or "hard" to indicate if the letter "c" makes the soft or hard sound.

	Sound "c" or "k"	"soft" or "hard"
1.	_____	_____
2.	_____	_____
3.	_____	_____
4.	_____	_____
5.	_____	_____
6.	_____	_____
7.	_____	_____
8.	_____	_____
9.	_____	_____
10.	_____	_____

The words listed below all begin with the letter "c." In four of the words, the "c" makes the **hard sound**. Circle the words that have the letter "c" making the hard sound. On the blanks that follow, write a sentence using each of the words in which "c" makes the hard sound.

| camp | card | city | census | cell | cart | cider | cube |

11. _____

12. _____

13. _____

14. _____

In the activity on the next page, write three words beginning with the letter "c" making the soft sound and three words with the letter "c" making the hard sound. Do not use any words from the above exercises. On the blank below each word, write a sentence

Name _____ Date _____

using each of the words beginning with "c." Circle **"hard"** or **"soft"** to indicate the sound the "c" makes.

15. word: _____ (hard/soft)

sentence: _____

16. word: _____ (hard/soft)

sentence: _____

17. word: _____ (hard/soft)

sentence: _____

18. word: _____ (hard/soft)

sentence: _____

19. word: _____ (hard/soft)

sentence: _____

20. word: _____ (hard/soft)

sentence: _____

In the reading selection below, some of the words in bold type begin with the soft sound of "c," and some begin with the hard sound of "c." Read the entire selection silently. Then reread the selection, and on the blanks below, write the words in bold that begin with the hard or soft sound of "c" on the appropriate lines.

Cal lay looking at the **ceiling** hoping that **Cindy** would **call**. Just then Champ, his **collie** dog, walked in and stared **calmly** at **Callie**, the family **cat**, who lay on a rug in the **center** of the room. Callie's attention was on the **cage** that hung from the ceiling and housed the **cinnamon-colored** parakeet. Callie knew that it would normally be dangerous to be so **casual** about Champ, but she **could** be **careless** with Cal present. Ignoring Callie, Champ approached Cal and began to **caress** his hand with his tongue.

The ringing of the phone **caught** Cal's attention. He **cautiously** picked up the phone and heard Cindy asking him to go to the **circus**. Quickly he hooked the leash to Champ's **collar** and ran from the house, stopping long enough for a piece of the **cake** his mother had left to **cool** in the **center** of their **cedar** table.

21. Hard sound: _____

_____

_____

22. Soft sound: _____

_____

Name _____ Date _____

| ACTIVITY 38 | THE SOFT AND HARD SOUNDS OF "g" |

You have learned that the letter "g" can make a soft or a hard sound. When "g" sounds like "g" in "gold," it is called **the hard sound of "g."** When the "g" makes a "j" sound, as in the word "gym," it is called **the soft sound.**

For the following activity, your teacher will pronounce words that all begin with the letter "g." The sound heard at the beginning of some of the words will be the "j" sound heard in "gym." In other words, the sound will be the "g" sound heard in "gold." After a word is pronounced, write the letter **"g"** or **"j"** below to show the sound you hear at the beginning of each word. Then write **"hard"** or **"soft"** to indicate if the letter "g" makes the hard or soft sound.

Sound "g" or "j"	"hard" or "soft"
1. _____	_____
2. _____	_____
3. _____	_____
4. _____	_____
5. _____	_____
6. _____	_____
7. _____	_____
8. _____	_____
9. _____	_____
10. _____	_____

All of the words below begin with the letter "g." In four of the words, the "g" makes the "j" or soft sound. Circle the words that have the soft sound of "g." On the blanks below, write sentences correctly using each of the words where the "g" makes the soft sound.

germ   gold   glass   gentle   genie   good   green   gem

11. _____

12. _____

13. _____

14. _____

Name _____ Date _____

Four of the words below have the hard sound of "g." Underline the words that have the letter "g" making the hard sound. On the blanks below, write sentences correctly using each of the words where the "g" makes the hard sound.

germ   gold   glass   gentle   genie   good   green   gem

15. _____

16. _____

17. _____

18. _____

Some of the words in bold type in the selection below have the soft sound of "g," and some have the hard sound of "g." Read the entire selection silently. Then reread the selection, and on the appropriate lines below, write the words in bold that have the hard or soft sound of "g."

George stood looking at the **orange** and **cabbage** behind the **glass** window. The orange was a bright **gold** color, and the **large green** cabbage looked fresh. The orange, cabbage, and a **gallon** of milk would complete the shopping list for his mother. Even though George was missing the **game**, he was **glad** to shop today for his mother. She was at home cooking the **goose** that the **judges** would eat to determine the **program** winner.

19. Words with the hard sound: _____

_____

20. Words with the soft sound: _____

_____

Name _____ Date _____

ACTIVITY 39 | RULES FOR SOFT OR HARD "c" OR "g"

You have learned how the letters "c" and "g" may have a hard or soft sound. The following rules may be used to determine if the letters "c" and "g" make the "soft" or "hard" sound at the beginning of a word.

1. When the letter "c" or "g" is followed by **"e," "i,"** or **"y,"** the **soft sound** is used: the "s" sound for "c" (city) and the "j" sound for "g" (gym).

2. When the letter "c" or "g" is followed by **"o," "a,"** or **"u,"** the **hard sound** is used: the "k" sound for "c" (cat) and the "g" sound for "g" (game).

Refer to the above rules and place each of the following words on the appropriate line below.

cycle	cent	ginger	gypsy	capital	camp
came	city	certain	cyclone	gallon	gallop
gyp	gently	geography	canoe	calm	gate
gem	giant	gab	general	candy	cane
cell	cider	gave	germ	center	canyon

1. Words beginning with the letter "g" with the hard sound: _____

_____

_____

2. Words beginning with the letter "g" with the soft sound: _____

_____

_____

3. Words beginning with the letter "c" with the hard sound: _____

_____

_____

4. Words beginning with the letter "c" with the soft sound: _____

_____

_____

Name _____ Date _____

ACTIVITY 40 LEARNING ABOUT THE SOUNDS OF THE LETTER "X"

The letter "**x**" stands for different sounds in different words. The letter "x" may stand for the sounds **/ks/, /gz/,** or **/z/**. In the word "**sox,**" you hear "so(**ks**)." In the word "**exit,**" you hear "e(**gz**)it." In the word "**xerox,**" you hear "(**z**)erox."

Below are words with the letter "x." Place each of the words in the column that represents the sound "x" makes in the word.

box	xylem	xenon	extension	xylophone
fox	toxic	xebec	exert	explain

1. **sox (ks)**	2. **exit (gz)**	3. **xerox (z)**
_____	_____	_____
_____	_____	_____
_____	_____	_____
_____	_____	_____
_____	_____	_____

The letter "x" presents an exception to the pattern **VCV** for dividing words into syllables. Normally, when a word fits the VCV pattern, the syllable is divided before the consonant. When the letter "x" is in the VCV pattern, the syllable division comes after the letter "x."

Examples:

Usual syllable division for VCV pattern: **ego   e/go**
Division for syllables with the letter "x": **exit   ex/it**

Divide each of the following words into syllables and give the sound "x" makes in the word.

Word	Syllable Division	Dictionary Pronunciation	Sound of "x"
4. exert	_____		_____
5. exam	_____		_____
6. exalt	_____		_____
7. exempt	_____		_____
8. exist	_____		_____
9. exude	_____		_____
10. execute	_____		_____

Name _____ Date _____

ACTIVITY 41 LEARNING ABOUT THE SOUNDS OF THE LETTER "q"

The letter **"q"** is always followed by the letter **"u."** The letters **"qu"** act as a single consonant when used in words. The letters "qu" are sounded as **/kw/** or **/k/** in words.

Examples: The "qu" in "quick" is pronounced /kw/. (kw) ick
             The "qu" in "unique" is pronounced /k/. uni(k)e

In pronouncing each of the following words, the "qu" should be given the /k/ or /kw/ sound. Answer the questions for each word. Pronounce the word and then write a sentence correctly using the word pronounced.

1. quack

a. This word has _____ syllable(s).

b. The word has a(n) (open/closed) syllable.

c. The sound used for the vowel is the (short/long) sound.

d. The letters "ck" are a (digraph/blend).

e. The sound for "qu" is (/k/, /kw/).

Sentence: _____

2. quick

a. This word has _____ syllable(s).

b. The word has a(n) (open/closed) syllable.

c. The sound used for the vowel is the (short/long) sound.

d. The letters "ck" are a (digraph/blend)

e. The sound for "qu" is (/k/, /kw/).

Sentence: _____

3. quake

a. This word has _____ syllable(s).

b. The word has a(n) (open/closed) syllable.

c. The vowel sounded is the vowel (u/a).

d. The sound used for the vowel is the (short/long) sound.

e. The letter "e" is (sounded/silent).

 f. The sound for "qu" is (/k/, /kw/).

Sentence: _____

Name _____ Date _____

ACTIVITY 41 LEARNING ABOUT THE SOUNDS OF THE LETTER "q" (CONT.)

4. quote

a. This word has _____ syllable(s).

b. This word has a(n) (open/closed) syllable.

c. The vowel sounded is the vowel (u/o).

d. The sound used for the vowel is the (short/long) sound.

e. The letter "e" is (sounded/silent).

f. The sound for "qu" is (/k/, /kw/).

Sentence: _____

5. equal

a. This word has _____ syllable(s).

b. The first syllable is a(n) (open/closed) syllable.

c. The vowel sounded in the first syllable is the vowel (e/a).

d. The sound used for the vowel in the second syllable is the (short/long) sound.

e. The letter "e" is (sounded/silent).

f. The sound for "qu" is (/k/, /kw/).

Sentence: _____

6. quarrel

a. This word has _____ syllable(s).

b. The first syllable is a(n) (open/closed) syllable.

c. The vowel sounded in the first syllable is controlled by the letter____ .

d. The sound for "qu" is (/k/, /kw/).

Sentence: _____

7. antique (give the letter "i" the sound for long "e")

a. This word has _____ syllable(s).

b. The vowel sound for the letter "a" will be (short/long).

c. The letter "e" is (sounded/silent).

d. The sound for "qu" is (/k/, /kw/).

Sentence: _____

Name _____ Date _____

ACTIVITY 42 IDENTIFYING THE SOUND OF "q"

Read the following selection silently. Then read it a second time. In the blank by each of the bold words, place the letters "k" or "kw" to indicate the sound made by the letters "qu" in the word.

The **queen** (1) _____ stood in the **quad** (2)_____, surrounded by the royal buildings,

and read the **request** (3)_____ for ships from the sailor. Some said he was a **quack**

(4) _____who wanted to explore a new route to the East. In the letter the sailor indicated

that he had no **qualms** (5) _____ about the success of the voyage. In fact, he was so sure

of success that this first trip would be one of a **sequence** (6)_____ of voyages. He was not

asking for a **squadron** (7)_____ of ships, only three. He would not **quibble** (8) _____ over

sharing **equal** (9)_____ parts of any **quantity** (10) _____ of the fortunes he might find.

In fact, he was willing to give the queen **quintuple** (11)_____ the **quantity** (12)_____he

might claim from the exploration.

The sailor indicated that he had a **quintet** (13) _____ of reliable officers who would

share the **quarterdeck** (14)_____ and **squeeze** (15)_____ a full day's work from the crew.

These officers knew exactly how to **equip** (16) _____the ships. Each crew member would

receive a **quid** (17) _____ and a **quart** (18)_____ of rum.

The queen stopped and placed her hand on the **grotesque** (19)_____ statue that

graced the quad. It was an **antique**, (20)_____ so she allowed it to be placed where a

more **picturesque** (21)_____ work of art would be more appealing.

The **quill** (22)_____in the queen's hand did not **quiver** (23)_____as she wrote

the sailor's answer. He must make his request to the king and **quote** (24)_____ the

benefits of the voyage to the king. The **equity** (25)_____ of the king's judgment would

be his best hope for help.

Name _____ Date _____

Learning About Silent Letters

ACTIVITY 43	**LEARNING ABOUT SILENT LETTERS: "g"**

You are familiar with the fact that the letter "e" is often silent when pronouncing a word. There are other letters that are not always pronounced when they appear in a word. The letters **"g," "gh," "k," "l," "p," "t,"** and **"w"** are sometimes silent.

When the letters "gn" appear in a word, the "g" is silent.
Example: **"gnat"** is pronounced **/nat/**

On the blanks beside each word, write the letters that are pronounced when reading the word. Then answer the questions that follow each word. Write a sentence correctly using the word on the blank that follows the questions.

1. **gnash**   _ _ _ _
   a. The word is a(n) (open/closed) syllable.
   b. The sound of the letter "a" is (long/short).
   c. The letters "sh" form a (digraph/blend).
   d. The letters "sh" (form a new sound/are both pronounced) in the word "gnash."
   e. Sentence: _____

2. **gnu**   _ _
   a. The word is a(n) (open/closed) syllable.
   b. The sound of the letter "u" is (short/long).
   c. Sentence: _____

3. **gnarl**   _ _ _ _
   a. The word is a(n) (open/closed) syllable.
   b. The vowel sound is (long/short/schwa/r-controlled).
   c. Sentence: _____

4. **gnome**   _ _ _
   a. The word is a(n) (open/closed) syllable.
   b. The vowel is (long/short/schwa/r-controlled).
   c. The letters _____ and ____ are silent in this word.
   d. Sentence: _____

5. **gnostic**   _ _ _ _ _ _
   a. The word has _____ syllables.
   b. The syllables are (open/closed).
   c. The vowel in the first syllable is (short/long/schwa/r-controlled).
   d. The vowel in the second syllable is (short/long/schwa/r-controlled).
   e. The syllable division is between the letters____ and ____.
   f. Sentence: _____

Name _____ Date _____

| ACTIVITY 44 | LEARNING ABOUT SILENT LETTERS: "k" |

When the letters "kn" appear in a word, the "k" is silent. On the blanks beside each word, write the letters that are pronounced when reading the word. Then answer the questions that follow each word. Write a sentence correctly using the word on the blank that follows the questions.

1. **knife**   _ _ _
   a. The syllable is (open/closed).
   b. The vowel sound in the word is made by the letter ____ .
   c. The vowel sound in the word is (long/short/schwa/r-controlled).
   d. The silent letters in the word are ____ and ____ .
   e. Sentence: _____

2. **knead**   _ _ _
   a. The syllable is (open/closed).
   b. The vowel sound in the word is made by the letter ____ .
   c. The vowel sound in the word is (long/short/schwa/r-controlled).
   d. The silent letters in the word are ____ and ____ .
   e. Sentence: _____

3. **knuckle** _ _ _ _ _
   a. The word has _____ syllable(s).
   b. The vowel sound in the word is made by the letter ____ .
   c. The vowel sound in the word is (long/short/schwa/r-controlled).
   d. The silent letters in the word are the letters ____ and ____ .
   e. Sentence: _____

4. **knee**   _ _
   a. The syllable is (open/closed).
   b. The vowel sound in the word is made by the letter ____ .
   c. The vowel sound in the word is (long/short/schwa/r-controlled).
   d. The silent letters in the word are ____ and ____ .
   e. Sentence: _____

5. **knapsack** _ _ _ _ _ _ _
   a. The syllables in the word are (open/closed).
   b. The vowel sounds in the word are made by the letter ____ .
   c. The vowel sounds in the word are (long/short/schwa/r-controlled).
   d. The silent letters in the word are ____ and ____ .
   e. Sentence: _____

Name _____ Date _____

ACTIVITY 45   LEARNING ABOUT SILENT LETTERS: "l"

      The letter "l" is silent when it appears before the letters "m," "d," or "k." On the blanks below, write the letters that are pronounced when reading each of the following words. Answer the questions following each word. Then write a sentence correctly using the word on the blank that follows the questions.

1. **calm**   _ _ _
   a. The word has _____ syllable(s).
   b. The syllable(s) is/are (open/closed).
   c. The vowel(s) in the word is/are ___ .
   d. The vowel sound in the word is (long/short/schwa/r-controlled).
   e. The silent letter in the word is ____ .
   f. Sentence: _____

2. **would**   _ _ _ _
   a. The word has _____ syllable(s).
   b. The syllable(s) is/are (open/closed).
   c. The vowel(s) in the word are the letters ___ and ___ .
   d. The silent letter in the word is ____ .
   e. Sentence: _____

3. **walk**   _ _ _
   a. The word has _____ syllable(s).
   b. The syllable(s) is/are (open/closed).
   c. The vowel in the word is ___ .
   d. The silent letter in the word is ___ .
   e. Sentence: _____

4. **chalk**   _ _ _ _
   a. The word has _____ syllable(s).
   b. The syllable(s) is/are (open/closed).
   c. The vowel in the word is ____ .
   d. The silent letter in the word is ___ .
   e. Sentence: _____

Name _____ Date _____

ACTIVITY 46 LEARNING ABOUT SILENT LETTERS: "gh"

The letters "gh" are silent when they appear in the middle or at the end of many words. On the blanks below, write the letters that are pronounced when reading each of the following words. Answer the questions following each word. Then write a sentence correctly using the word on the blank that follows the questions.

1. **high** _ _
   a. The silent letters in the word are ___ and ___.
   b. The vowel in the word is the letter ___.
   c. Because "gh" is silent, the syllable is (open/closed).
   d. The sound of the vowel is (long/short).
   e. Sentence: _____

2. **fighter** _ _ _ _ _
   a. The silent letters in the word are ___ and ___.
   b. The vowels in the word are the letters ___ and ___.
   c. The sound of the vowel ___ in the word is controlled by the letter "r."
   d. Because the "gh" is silent, the first syllable is (open/closed).
   e. The sound of the vowel in the first syllable is (long/short).
   f. Sentence: _____

3. **taught** _ _ _ _
   a. The silent letters in the word are ___ and ___.
   b. The vowels in the word are the letters ___ and ___.
   c. The vowel sound is the same as the vowel sound in the word (tan/sun/caught).
   d. Sentence: _____

4. **sight** _ _ _
   a. The silent letters in the word are ___ and ___.
   b. The vowel in the word is the letter ___.
   c. The vowel sound is (long/short).
   d. The syllable is (open/closed).
   e. Sentence: _____

Name _____ Date _____

ACTIVITY 47 LEARNING ABOUT SILENT LETTERS: "t"

The letter "t" is silent before "en" and "le." On the blanks below, write the letters that are pronounced when reading each of the following words. Answer the questions following each word. Then write a sentence correctly using the word on the blank that follows the questions.

1. **listen**   _ _ _ _ _
   a. The word has _____ syllable(s).
   b. The first syllable is (open/closed).
   c. The vowels in the word are ___ and ___ .
   d. The vowel sound in the first syllable is (long/short/schwa/r-controlled).
   e. The vowel sound in the second syllable is (long/short/schwa/r-controlled).
   f. The silent letter in the word is the letter ___ .
   g. Sentence: _____

2. **often**   _ _ _ _
   a. The word has_____ syllable(s).
   b. The first syllable is (open/closed).
   c. The vowels in the word are ___ and ___ .
   d. The vowel sound in the first syllable is (long/short/schwa/r-controlled).
   e. The vowel sound in the second syllable is (long/short/schwa/r-controlled).
   f. The silent letter in the word is the letter ___ .
   g. Sentence: _____

3. **thistle**   _ _ _ _ _ _
   a. The word has _____ syllable(s).
   b. The syllable division is between the letters ___ and ___ .
   c. The first syllable is (open/closed).
   d. The vowels in the word are ___ and ___ .
   e. The vowel sound in the first syllable is (long/short/schwa/r-controlled).
   f. The silent letter in this word is the letter ___ .
   g. Sentence: _____

4. **castle**   _ _ _ _ _
   a. The word has_____ syllable(s).
   b. The syllable division is between the letters ___ and ___ .
   c. The first syllable is (open/closed).
   d. The vowels in the word are ___ and ___ .
   e. The vowel sound in the first syllable is (long/short/schwa/r-controlled).
   f. The silent letter in this word is the letter ___ .
   g. Sentence: _____

Name _____ Date _____

ACTIVITY 48 LEARNING ABOUT SILENT LETTERS: "W"

The letter "w" is silent before the letter "r." On the blanks below, write the letters that are pronounced when reading each of the following words. Answer the questions following each word. Then write a sentence correctly using the word on the blank that follows the questions.

1. **write**   _ _ _
   a. The word has _____ syllable(s).
   b. The syllable(s) is/are (open/closed).
   c. The vowels in the word are ___ and ___.
   d. The vowel sound in the word is (long/short/schwa/r-controlled).
   e. The silent letters in the word are ___ and ___.
   f. Sentence: _____

2. **wrist**   _ _ _ _
   a. The word has _____ syllable(s).
   b. The syllable(s) is/are (open/closed).
   c. The vowel in the word is ___.
   d. The vowel sound in the word is (long/short/schwa/r-controlled).
   e. The silent letter in the word is ___.
   f. The letters "st" at the end of the word are a (blend/digraph).
   g. Sentence: _____

3. **wrapper** _ _ _ _ _ _
   a. The word has _____ syllable(s).
   b. The syllable(s) is/are (open/closed).
   c. The vowels in the word are the letter ___ and the r-controlled ___.
   d. The vowel sound in the first syllable is (long/short/schwa/r-controlled).
   e. The silent letter in the word is the letter ___.
   f. Sentence: _____

4. **wreckage** _ _ _ _ _ _ _ _
   a. The word has _____ syllable(s).
   b. The first syllable is (open/closed).
   c. The second syllable is the letters _ _ _ .
   d. The vowel sound in the first syllable is (long/short/schwa/r-controlled).
   e. The silent letters in the word are the consonants ___ and ___ and the vowel ___.
   f. Sentence: _____

Name _____ Date _____

ACTIVITY 59	LEARNING ABOUT SUFFIXES

Many suffixes change the root word to show possession, change the root to the plural form, change the verb tense of the root, or change the root to the comparative or superlative form of the adjective.

The following words are root words with suffixes added to the end of the word. Place the root word in the blank under the Root heading. Then, write each suffix in the blank under the appropriate heading that describes how the suffix has changed the root.

Word	Root	Possession	Plural	Tense Change	Degree Change
1. boys	_____	_____	_____	_____	_____
2. boy's	_____	_____	_____	_____	_____
3. baby's	_____	_____	_____	_____	_____
4. men's	_____	_____	_____	_____	_____
5. singing	_____	_____	_____	_____	_____
6. tallest	_____	_____	_____	_____	_____
7. brushes	_____	_____	_____	_____	_____
8. lamps	_____	_____	_____	_____	_____
9. played	_____	_____	_____	_____	_____
10. calmer	_____	_____	_____	_____	_____

Add a suffix to each of the following words (roots). On the blank, tell how the suffix changes the root word.

Root	Root With Suffix	Explain How Suffix Changed Root
11. fast	_____	_____
12. park	_____	_____
13. eat	_____	_____
14. jump	_____	_____
15. fill	_____	_____

Adding a suffix may change an adjective to an adverb or to a comparative or superlative adjective. Add the suffixes "er" or "est" and "ly" to each root, and write the adjective and adverb on the blanks under the proper heading.

Root	Comp./Super. Adjective	Suffix Added	Adverb	Suffix Added
16. quick	_____	_____	_____	_____
17. short	_____	_____	_____	_____
18. slow	_____	_____	_____	_____
19. quiet	_____	_____	_____	_____
20. swift	_____	_____	_____	_____

Name _____ Date _____

ACTIVITY 60 | WHAT SUFFIXES DO

Suffixes are added to the ends of root words. A suffix is usually a separate syllable that changes the word to a different part of speech or makes the meaning of the word clearer. The suffixes **"s," "ed," "ing," "er,"** and **"est"** usually **make the meaning of a word clearer.** Suffixes like **"ful," "ness," "less," "ly," "er,"** and **"ist"** often **change a word to another part of speech.**

Example: The meaning of the word **"dog"** is made clearer by adding **"s,"** so the word becomes **"dogs."** It does not change the part of speech of the word.

The **dogs** ran after the fox. (Adding the **"s"** tells the reader that there was more than one dog.

Example: The verb **"play"** is changed to an adjective by adding the suffix **"ful"** to make the word **"playful."**

The dog was in a **playful** mood. (Adding **"ful"** makes **"playful"** an adjective that describes the dog's mood.

Each of the words below has a suffix. Write the suffix on the blank next to the word. Place a check mark on the blank that indicates whether the suffix changes the part of speech of the root word or if it more clearly defines the meaning of the root word. Then write a sentence using the root word and a sentence using the root word with the suffix.

1. **hopeless** _____ ___Changes part of speech   ___ Makes meaning clearer

Sentence: _____

Sentence: _____

2. **smallest** _____ ___Changes part of speech   ___ Makes meaning clearer

Sentence: _____

Sentence: _____

3. **sadly** _____ ___Changes part of speech   ___ Makes meaning clearer

Sentence: _____

Sentence: _____

4. **latest** _____ ___Changes part of speech   ___ Makes meaning clearer

Sentence: _____

Sentence: _____

5. **careful** _____ ___Changes part of speech   ___ Makes meaning clearer

Sentence: _____

Sentence: _____

Name _____ Date _____

ACTIVITY 60 WHAT SUFFIXES DO (CONTINUED)

6. **classify** _____ __ Changes part of speech   __ Makes meaning clearer

Sentence: _____

Sentence: _____

7. **attractive** _____ __ Changes part of speech   __ Makes meaning clearer

Sentence: _____

Sentence: _____

8. **faithful** _____ __ Changes part of speech   __ Makes meaning clearer

Sentence: _____

Sentence: _____

9. **flawless** _____ __ Changes part of speech   __ Makes meaning clearer

Sentence: _____

Sentence: _____

10. **childish** _____ __ Changes part of speech   __ Makes meaning clearer

Sentence: _____

Sentence: _____

11. **manly** _____ __ Changes part of speech   __ Makes meaning clearer

Sentence: _____

Sentence: _____

12. **minority** _____ __ Changes part of speech   __ Makes meaning clearer

Sentence: _____

Sentence: _____

13. **construction** _____ __ Changes part of speech   __ Makes meaning clearer

Sentence: _____

Sentence: _____

14. **acceptable** _____ __ Changes part of speech   __ Makes meaning clearer

Sentence: _____

Sentence: _____

15. **idealism** _____ __ Changes part of speech   __ Makes meaning clearer

Sentence: _____

Sentence: _____

Name _____ Date _____

ACTIVITY 61 LEARNING MORE ABOUT SUFFIXES

Add one of the suffixes below to each of the following roots to make a new word. On the line below each root, write a sentence using the new word.

able	ish	ment	ly	less
ic	er	y	ful	

Root   **Root With Suffix**

1. rain   _____

Sentence: _____

2. home   _____

Sentence: _____

3. depend   _____

Sentence: _____

4. care   _____

Sentence: _____

5. work   _____

Sentence: _____

6. sad   _____

Sentence: _____

7. fool   _____

Sentence: _____

8. excite   _____

Sentence: _____

9. hero   _____

Sentence: _____

10. self   _____

Sentence: _____

Name _____ Date _____

ACTIVITY 62 | HOW SUFFIXES CHANGE THE SPELLING OF ROOTS

Sometimes when a suffix is added to a word, the spelling of the root word is changed. Read the root word in the first column, and then read the root with the suffix added in the second column. On the blank, tell how the root was changed by the suffix.

Root	Root and Suffix	How Root Was Changed
1. happy	happiness	_____
2. lonely	loneliness	_____
3. easy	easily	_____
4. duty	duties	_____
5. try	tried	_____

Look closely at the above roots and answer the following questions.

6. Each of the above words ended with the letter_____ .

7. In each word, the letter before the "y" is a (consonant/vowel).

8. In each word, when the suffix was added, the letter_____ in the root was dropped.

9. When a root ends in the letter (a) _____with a (b) (consonant/vowel) before it, the letter
   (c) _____ is changed to the letter (d)_____ , and the suffix is added.

Use the suffixes below and add one to each of the following roots.

iest	ied	iful	iness

10. tiny _____

11. cheery _____

12. multiply _____

13. beauty _____

15. happy _____

When **"ed"** or **"ing"** is added to a base word that ends in a single consonant, the consonant is usually doubled to preserve the short sound of the base.

Example: **"grab"** = **"grabbed"** not **"grabed"**   **"hop"** = **"hopping"** not **"hoping"**

Add the suffix "ed" or "ing" to each of the root words below. Write the new word on the blank next to the base word.

16. cap _____   17. stop _____   18. bat _____

19. drop _____   20. stab _____

Name _____   Date _____

ACTIVITY 63 | HOW SUFFIXES CHANGE THE SPELLING OF ROOTS

Read the root in Column A, and then read the root with the suffix added in Column B. Answer the questions below.

Column A   **Column B**

1. play   playing
2. boy   boyish
3. joy   joyful
4. stay   stayed

5. Each of the above roots ended with the letter_____.

6. In each word, the letter before the "y" is a (consonant/vowel).

7. When a root ends in the letter (a)____ with a (b) (consonant/vowel) before it, the suffix is added without any change in the root.

Use the suffixes below and add one to each of the following roots.

              ed   **ful**   **ing**   **ment**

8. say _____   9. deploy _____   10. enjoy _____   11. stray _____

You are learning that the letter "y" at the end of a word is a signal when adding suffixes. The following activity includes a list of words that will give you another signal when adding a suffix to words that end with the letter "y." Refer to the three words in bold, and answer the questions that follow.

              carry   **satisfy**   **reply**

12. Each of the words ends with the letter_____.

13. In each word, the letter "y" has a (consonant/vowel) before the letter "y."

Refer to the following words and answer the questions that follow.

              carrying   **satisfying**   **replying**

14. Each of the words has the suffix _____ added to the word.

15. Were any letters dropped before adding the suffix? (yes/no)

16. The suffix begins with the letter_____ .

Add the suffix **"ing"** to each of the following words and write the word on the blank.

17. hurry _____   18. fly _____   19. try _____

20. When a word ends with the letter "y" with a consonant before the letter "y" and the suffix begins with the letter (a)_____, the word (b) (is/is not) changed before adding the (c)_____.

Name _____ Date _____

ACTIVITY 64 | HOW SUFFIXES CHANGE THE SPELLING OF ROOTS

Draw a line from the root in Column A to that root with a suffix in Column B.

Column A	Column B
1. excite	A. ration
2. rate	B. movable
3. move	C. exciting
4. note	D. desired
5. receive	E. notable
6. desire	F. receiving

Refer to the words above and answer the following questions.

7. Each of the above roots in Column A ends with the letter _____.

8. Each of the suffixes added begins with a (consonant/vowel).

9. In each root, the letter _____ was dropped.

10. When a root ends in the letter (a)_____ and the suffix added begins with a (b) (consonant/vowel), the letter (c)_____ in the root is dropped.

When reading you will often come to a word with a suffix and be unable to pronounce the word. If you can determine what the root word is, you will often be able to pronounce the unknown word. The next activity will help you to identify root words.

Each of the following words is made from a root and a suffix. In some words, the root was not changed. In other words, letters were dropped before the suffix was added. Write the root word for each word on the blank.

11. enjoyable _____

12. girlish _____

13. smiling _____

14. desired _____

15. exciting _____

16. completely _____

17. skinniest _____

18. atmospheric _____

19. wonderful _____

20. botanist _____

Name _____ Date _____

ACTIVITY 65 ROOT WORDS AND SUFFIXES

You have learned that a root word may or may not be changed when a suffix is added. In the following activity, suffixes have been added to words. Use a dictionary, if necessary, to identify the part of speech of the word and use it correctly in a sentence. Then write the root word on the appropriate blank, identify the part of speech of the root, and use it correctly in a sentence.

1. **wickedness**   Part of Speech: _____
Sentence: _____
Root Word: _____ Part of Speech: _____
Sentence: _____

2. **attraction**   Part of Speech: _____
Sentence: _____
Root Word: _____ Part of Speech: _____
Sentence: _____

3. **expensive**   Part of Speech: _____
Sentence: _____
Root Word: _____ Part of Speech: _____
Sentence: _____

4. **loyalist**   Part of Speech: _____
Sentence: _____
Root Word: _____ Part of Speech: _____
Sentence: _____

5. **lovable**   Part of Speech: _____
Sentence: _____
Root Word: _____ Part of Speech: _____
Sentence: _____

6. **creamery**   Part of Speech: _____
Sentence: _____
Root Word: _____ Part of Speech: _____
Sentence: _____

7. **difference**   Part of Speech: _____
Sentence: _____
Root Word: _____ Part of Speech: _____
Sentence: _____

Name _____ Date _____

ACTIVITY 65 ROOT WORDS AND SUFFIXES (CONTINUED)

8. **penniless**   Part of Speech: _____

Sentence: _____

Root Word: _____ Part of Speech: _____

Sentence: _____

9. **commercial**   Part of Speech: _____

Sentence: _____

Root Word: _____ Part of Speech: _____

Sentence: _____

10. **stationary**   Part of Speech: _____

Sentence: _____

Root Word: _____ Part of Speech: _____

Sentence: _____

11. **enclosure**   Part of Speech: _____

Sentence: _____

Root Word: _____ Part of Speech: _____

Sentence: _____

12. **prosperous**   Part of Speech: _____

Sentence: _____

Root Word: _____ Part of Speech: _____

Sentence: _____

13. **allowance**   Part of Speech: _____

Sentence: _____

Root Word: _____ Part of Speech: _____

Sentence: _____

14. **historic**   Part of Speech: _____

Sentence: _____

Root Word: _____ Part of Speech: _____

Sentence: _____

15. **narration**   Part of Speech: _____

Sentence: _____

Root Word: _____ Part of Speech: _____

Sentence: _____

Name _____ Date _____

ACTIVITY 66 IDENTIFYING ROOTS AND SUFFIXES

Read the following selection. Find the root word for each word in boldface type. Write the root for each word on the blank next to the word.

The **national** (1)_____ budget of the United States is **basically** (2) _____ a **commitment** (3) _____ to the citizens. The budget includes **monetary** (4) _____ **obligations** (5) _____ for **protection** (6)_____ , **education** (7) _____ , and **enforcement** (8) _____. The **distribution** (9) _____ of money to the states for **employment** (10)_____ purposes is based on the individual **prosperity** (11) _____ of the states. The individual cities in the states raise **additional** (12)_____ money for their needs by **taxation** (13)_____ on the **commercial** (14)_____ and **residential** (15) _____ properties within cities.

Each of the highlighted words from the above selection is listed in Column A below. In Column B is a meaning that matches the suffix as it is used in the above selection. Match the meaning of the suffix from Column B with the appropriate words in Column A.

Column A

_____ 16. national

_____ 17. basically

_____ 18. commitment

_____ 19. monetary

_____ 20. obligations

_____ 21. protection

_____ 22. education

_____ 23. enforcement

_____ 24. distribution

_____ 25. employment

_____ 26. prosperity

_____ 27. additional

_____ 28. taxation

_____ 29. commercial

_____ 30. residential

Column B

A. the act of

B. relating to

C. state of being

D. like or characteristic of

80

Name _____ Date _____

Learning About Structural Analysis: Prefixes

ACTIVITY 67	LEARNING ABOUT PREFIXES

In the previous activities using suffixes, you have learned that a suffix is added to the end of a root word. **A prefix is added to the beginning of a root word.**

Examples: **repay**   The root word is "**pay**," and the prefix is "**re**."
            indirect   The root word is "**direct**," and the prefix is "**in**."

In the activity below, each word has a prefix. Write the root word and the prefix on the blanks next to each word. On the line below each word, write a sentence correctly using the word.

	Root Word	**Prefix**
1. **unhappy**	_____	_____

Sentence: _____

| 2. **depart** | _____ | _____ |

Sentence: _____

| 3. **recall** | _____ | _____ |

Sentence: _____

| 4. **disagree** | _____ | _____ |

Sentence: _____

| 5. **uneven** | _____ | _____ |

Sentence: _____

| 6. **disorder** | _____ | _____ |

Sentence: _____

| 7. **enclose** | _____ | _____ |

Sentence: _____

| 8. **repair** | _____ | _____ |

Sentence: _____

| 9. **uncertain** | _____ | _____ |

Sentence: _____

| 10. **enlarge** | _____ | _____ |

Sentence: _____

| 11. **imprint** | _____ | _____ |

Sentence: _____

| 12. **intake** | _____ | _____ |

Sentence: _____

| 13. **nonstop** | _____ | _____ |

Sentence: _____

Name _____ Date _____

ACTIVITY 68 WHAT PREFIXES DO

Prefixes are separate syllables attached to the front of a word.
Example: **replay**   The prefix **"re"** is added to the front of the word "play."
Example: **disagree** The prefix **"dis"** is added to the front of the word "agree."

A prefix changes the meaning of a word or makes the meaning clearer.
Example: **replay**   The prefix **"re"** changes the word to mean "play again" or "play over."
Example: **disagree** The prefix **"dis"** changes the word to mean "not agree."

Each of the words below has a prefix. Write the prefix on the blank next to the word. On the lines below the word, write a sentence using the word with the prefix and a sentence using just the root word without the prefix.

1. **disconnect**   _____
Sentence: _____
Sentence: _____

2. **improper**   _____
Sentence: _____
Sentence: _____

3. **mismatch**   _____
Sentence: _____
Sentence: _____

4. **repay**   _____
Sentence: _____
Sentence: _____

5. **replace**   _____
Sentence: _____
Sentence: _____

6. **unequal**   _____
Sentence: _____
Sentence: _____

7. **incorrect**   _____
Sentence: _____
Sentence: _____

8. **disadvantage** _____
Sentence: _____
Sentence: _____

Name _____ Date _____

ACTIVITY 69 USING PREFIXES

Listed below are some prefixes that are very useful in reading and writing. A list of root words is also included below. On the blank by each root word, make a new word using one of the prefixes. Then, using only one word, complete the meaning for the new word.

in   im   ir   il   un   re   dis   over   mis

Root Word	New Word With Prefix	Meaning of New Word
1. polite	_____	not _____
2. decent	_____	not _____
3. secure	_____	not _____
4. pure	_____	not _____
5. spell	_____	_____ wrong
6. fair	_____	not _____
7. understand	_____	_____ wrong
8. regular	_____	not _____
9. react	_____	_____ too strongly
10. port	_____	bring _____
11. capable	_____	not _____
12. continue	_____	not _____
13. satisfied	_____	not _____
14. civilized	_____	not _____
15. rational	_____	not _____
16. legal	_____	not _____
17. apply	_____	_____ wrong
18. appropriate	_____	not _____
19. apply	_____	_____ again
20. pay	_____	_____ again

Name _____ Date _____

ACTIVITY 70 **PREFIX MATCHING**

Choose a prefix from Column B and place it on the blank before a word in Column A to make a new word. On the lines below, write a sentence using each new word.

Column A   **Column B**

1._____ cay   re

2._____ count   in

3._____ large   de

4._____ section   mis

5._____ attended   en

6._____ proper   dis

7._____ believe   im

8._____ attentive   inter

9._____ call   non

10._____ stop   un

Sentences:

11._____

12._____

13._____

14._____

15._____

16._____

17._____

18._____

19._____

20._____

Name _____   Date _____

ACTIVITY 71 USING PREFIXES IN TEXT

In the following selection, some words are highlighted. Remove the prefixes from the highlighted words to change the meaning of the selection. Rewrite the selection without the prefixes on the lines below.

The test was (1) **rescheduled** for Thursday. Mr. Jones was (2) **dissatisfied** with the (3) **irrational** responses students were giving to (4) **irrelevant** questions. Students were making (5) **incorrect** statements and (6) **misapplying** formulas when asked (7) **improbable** questions, which on the (8) **retest** were (9) **immaterial**.

_____

_____

_____

_____

_____

_____

_____

_____

_____

_____

In the following selection, add prefixes to the highlighted words to change the meaning of the selection. Select your prefixes from those listed below.

in   im   ir   il   un   re   dis   over   mis

The (10)_____ **orderly** students soon found that being (11)_____ **polite** in class had hurt their grades. Their (12)_____**behavior** was (13)_____ **appropriate**. Many students learned that the (14)_____ **appropriate** behavior was (15)_____**acceptable**, and they were asked to (16)_____ **continue**. Since they had (17)_____ **obeyed** and were (18)_____ **considerate**, it was their (19)_____ **fortune** to (20)_____ **take** the test.

Name _____ Date _____

ACTIVITY 72 | PRONOUNCING WORDS WITH PREFIXES

When a word has a prefix, the prefix is usually a separate syllable. When you are trying to determine the pronunciation of an unknown word, first take off any prefixes or suffixes the word may have. Then try to divide the word into syllables and use phonics to pronounce the word. You can then put the prefix back on the word and pronounce the word with the prefix.

Each of the following words has a prefix. Complete the blanks in the chart for each word. The first one is completed for you.

Word	Word Without Prefix	Syllable Division	Phonetic Spelling
1. mistake	take	mis/take	mĭ stāk′
2. inactive			
3. unhappy			
4. repaid			
5. impress			
6. enlarge			
7. insensitive			
8. discomfort			
9. untwist			
10. antiseptic			
11. intramuscular			
12. anticlimax			
13. destabilize			
14. inconsistent			
15. subdivide			

Name _____ Date _____

ACTIVITY 73 IDENTIFYING ROOT WORDS

Many times in reading, you will find words that you cannot pronounce. Recognizing the prefixes and suffixes can help you figure out what the word might be. When trying to sound out a word, it is important to take off any prefixes and suffixes before trying to sound out the word.

In the activity below is a list of words. Some have prefixes, some have suffixes, some have both, and some have neither. Complete the blanks for each word. Use a dictionary.

Word	Root Word	Phonetic Spelling	Prefix	Suffix
1. repayment	_____	_____	_____	_____
2. unsuccessful	_____	_____	_____	_____
3. rebuilt	_____	_____	_____	_____
4. nonconductor	_____	_____	_____	_____
5. meaningless	_____	_____	_____	_____
6. destructive	_____	_____	_____	_____
7. misapplication	_____	_____	_____	_____
8. immortal	_____	_____	_____	_____
9. direct	_____	_____	_____	_____
10. prehistoric	_____	_____	_____	_____
11. polite	_____	_____	_____	_____
12. fresh	_____	_____	_____	_____
13. cooperative	_____	_____	_____	_____
14. judgment	_____	_____	_____	_____
15. illiterate	_____	_____	_____	_____
16. unfounded	_____	_____	_____	_____
17. retract	_____	_____	_____	_____
18. mistaken	_____	_____	_____	_____
19. global	_____	_____	_____	_____
20. wrist	_____	_____	_____	_____

Name _____ Date _____

ACTIVITY 74 | REVIEWING HOW TO USE PREFIXES AND SUFFIXES

Add the prefix and suffix provided on each line to the root word to create a new word. Then write a sentence using the new word.

Root Word	Prefix	Suffix	New Word
1. **natural**	un	ly	_____

Sentence: _____

2. **circle**	semi	ular	_____

Sentence: _____

3. **sphere**	hemi	ical	_____

Sentence: _____

4. **respect**	dis	ful	_____

Sentence: _____

5. **nation**	inter	al	_____

Sentence: _____

6. **capture**	re	d	_____

Sentence: _____

7. **person**	im	al	_____

Sentence: _____

8. **diverse**	bio	ity	_____

Sentence: _____

9. **direct**	mis	ion	_____

Sentence: _____

10. **self**	un	ish	_____

Sentence: _____

Name _____ Date _____

Learning About Structural Analysis: Compound Words

ACTIVITY 75	LEARNING ABOUT COMPOUND WORDS

The following words are **compound words**. Write the two words that make the compound word on the appropriate blanks.

Compound Word   **Words Making the Compound Word**

1. policeman   _____   _____

2. fireplace   _____   _____

3. sidewalk   _____   _____

4. workshop   _____   _____

5. anybody   _____   _____

Each word in Column A can be matched with a word in Column B to make a compound word. Write the word from Column B on the blank next to the corresponding word in Column A. Then write the complete compound word.

Column A   **Compound Word**   **Column B**

6. rail   + _____ = _____   plane

7. street   + _____ = _____   bell

8. door   + _____ = _____   road

9. down   + _____ = _____   town

10. air   + _____ = _____   car

Place the letter of the definition in Column B on the line next to the correct compound word in Column A.

Column A   **Column B**

_____ 11. springtime   A. Where the fire is contained in a room

_____ 12. fireplace   B. The day of a person's birth

_____ 13. outside   C. Refers to a season of the year

_____ 14. downtown   D. The opposite of inside

_____ 15. birthday   E. The main part of a city

Name _____ Date _____

ACTIVITY 76 | DIVIDING COMPOUND WORDS INTO SYLLABLES

Divide each word below into syllables. Check your work using a dictionary. Rewrite each word on the blanks following each word. Under the column labeled Phonetic Spelling, write the word as it appears in the dictionary, showing all symbols that aid in pronouncing the word. Write the meaning of the word on the line below each word, and then write a sentence using the meaning selected.

Word	Syllable Division	Accented Syllable	Phonetic Spelling
1. downwind	_____	_____	_____

Meaning: _____

Sentence: _____

2. mainstream	_____	_____	_____

Meaning: _____

Sentence: _____

3. proofread	_____	_____	_____

Meaning: _____

Sentence: _____

4. landmass	_____	_____	_____

Meaning: _____

Sentence: _____

5. outlay	_____	_____	_____

Meaning: _____

Sentence: _____

6. Read the following selection silently. Then read it a second time and circle all of the compound words in the selection.

It was late afternoon in the springtime. He opened the curtains to let more sunlight into the bedroom. Checking his watch, he knew that he must hurry to catch the last streetcar to go downtown and shop for his sister's birthday. Coming downstairs, he noticed that his brother had left a basketball by the fireplace. He picked up the basketball and took it outside to the garage. Inside the garage, he placed the basketball in the cardboard box with the football and baseball. Just then he heard the streetcar bell and hurried out to get on board.

Name _____   Date _____

ACTIVITY 77 PHONETIC SPELLING OF COMPOUND WORDS

Read each of the following sentences. Compound words are shown with a phonetic spelling. Write the word on the blank following the phonetic spelling. On the line below the sentence, tell in your own words what the compound word means.

1. The [kē′nōt′] (_____) address was given by General Jones.
Meaning: _____

2. The young man was a [grēn′hôrn′] (_____) who was easy to fool.
Meaning: _____

3. He spoke for an hour and then added a [fōōt′nōt′] (_____) that did not relate to his speech.
Meaning: _____

4. Her new job required long hours of work, so finding a time to study created a real [härd′shĭp′] (_____).
Meaning: _____

5. Don't try to [hwīt′wôsh′] (_____) the error you have made.
Meaning: _____

6. It's better to tell your parents the truth, even if it gets you in the [dôg′hous′]
(_____).
Meaning: _____

7. If we don't get our assignments completed on time, there will be some real [fīr′wɹrks′]
(_____).
Meaning: _____

8. If we win the game, we will bring home the [härd′wĕr′] (_____).
Meaning: _____

9. I hope you don't try to [hăm′strĭng′] (_____) me in my efforts to win the office.
Meaning: _____

10. You must [hī′līt′] (_____) the main points in your speech to get your message across.
Meaning: _____

Name _____ Date _____

Learning About Structural Analysis: Accented Syllables

ACTIVITY 78 LEARNING ABOUT ACCENTED SYLLABLES

In the following activity, read each sentence. Determine the number of syllables in the boldface word. Then indicate the accented syllable. Fill in the chart below with that information after reading each sentence. Use a dictionary if needed.

1. He would not **accept** the award.

2. Chad began to **complain** that the test was too hard.

3. Christopher gave a good **reason** for not having the assignment.

4. He was **able** to solve the problem.

5. Chad's **polite** answer impressed the teacher.

6. The sun came over the **horizon** just as Christopher awoke.

7. The **material** Chad selected was blue with white stars.

8. It is not uncommon for logs to **petrify**.

9. Christopher's skin was **sensitive** to the summer sun.

10. After writing the letter, he addressed the **envelope**.

Word	Syllable Division	Number of Syllables	Accented Syllable
1. accept	_____	_____	_____
2. complain	_____	_____	_____
3. reason	_____	_____	_____
4. able	_____	_____	_____
5. polite	_____	_____	_____
6. horizon	_____	_____	_____
7. material	_____	_____	_____
8. petrify	_____	_____	_____
9. sensitive	_____	_____	_____
10. envelope	_____	_____	_____

Name _____ Date _____

ACTIVITY 79 CONTEXT, ACCENT, AND MEANING

You have learned that certain syllables are accented in a word. The way a word is pronounced and the syllable(s) accented often determine the meaning and part of speech of a word.

Example:
   re′cord   The accent is on the first syllable. In the sentence that follows, the accented first syllable makes the word a noun.
      The record (re′cord) will show that he has been late many times.

   re cord′   The accent is on the second syllable. In the sentence that follows, the accented syllable makes the word a verb.
      I will record (re cord′) the results as quickly as possible.

In this activity, you must pronounce each word twice. First, pronounce the word and place the accent on the first syllable. Then, complete the blanks that follow. Next, pronounce each word placing the accent on the second syllable and complete the blanks. Use a dictionary, if necessary. Write a sentence using the word as the part of speech indicated.

Word	Syllable Division	Accented Syllable	Part of Speech
1. a) **compound**	_____	_____	_____
b) **compound**	_____	_____	_____

noun: _____

verb: _____

| 2. a) **address** | _____ | _____ | _____ |
| b) **address** | _____ | _____ | _____ |

noun: _____

verb: _____

| 3. a) **transfer** | _____ | _____ | _____ |
| b) **transfer** | _____ | _____ | _____ |

noun: _____

verb: _____

| 4. a) **permit** | _____ | _____ | _____ |
| b) **permit** | _____ | _____ | _____ |

noun: _____

verb: _____

Name _____ Date _____

ACTIVITY 79 CONTEXT, ACCENT, AND MEANING (CONTINUED)

Word	Syllable Division	Accented Syllable	Part of Speech
5. a) **frequent**	_____	_____	_____
b) **frequent**	_____	_____	_____

adjective: _____

verb: _____

In the following, complete blanks "c" and "d" by indicating the part of speech before writing a sentence using the word as that part of speech.

6. a) **absent**	_____	_____	_____
b) **absent**	_____	_____	_____

c) _____ : _____

d) _____ : _____

7. a) **collect**	_____	_____	_____
b) **collect**	_____	_____	_____

c) _____ : _____

d) _____ : _____

8. a) **content**	_____	_____	_____
b) **content**	_____	_____	_____

c) _____ : _____

d) _____ : _____

9. a) **digest**	_____	_____	_____
b) **digest**	_____	_____	_____

c) _____ : _____

d) _____ : _____

10. a) **complex**	_____	_____	_____
b) **complex**	_____	_____	_____

c) _____ : _____

d) _____ : _____

Name _____ Date _____

ACTIVITY 80 THE SCHWA SOUND IN UNACCENTED SYLLABLES

In the unstressed syllable(s) of a word, the vowel is marked by the schwa sound. The schwa sound is the sound of a short "u." In the dictionary, the schwa sound is marked by the symbol ∂.

Example:

about (∂ bout′)   Note the unaccented syllable is "a." The sound of the "a" is like the short sound of "u." It is the schwa sound. Compare with the short sound of "u" in the word "nut."

pencil (pen′c∂l)   Note the unaccented syllable is "cil." The sound of the "i" is like the short sound of "u." It is the schwa sound. Compare with the short sound of "u" in the word "nut."

In the following activity, determine the accented and unaccented syllables. Complete the blanks for each word. Check your work using a dictionary.

Word	Syllable Division	Accented Syllable	Unaccented Syllable With Schwa Symbol
1. towel	_____	_____	_____
2. believe	_____	_____	_____
3. second	_____	_____	_____
4. delta	_____	_____	_____
5. element	_____	_____	_____

Find each of the following words in the dictionary. Indicate the accented and unaccented syllables. Write the dictionary pronunciation guide for each word, using the appropriate symbols. Then use each word in a sentence.

Word	Syllable Division	Accented Syllable	Unaccented Syllable(s)	Dictionary Pronunciation
6. congruity	_____	_____	_____	_____

Sentence: _____

| 7. gentry | _____ | _____ | _____ | _____ |

Sentence: _____

| 8. ineloquent | _____ | _____ | _____ | _____ |

Sentence: _____

| 9. production | _____ | _____ | _____ | _____ |

Sentence: _____

| 10. ulcerate | _____ | _____ | _____ | _____ |

Sentence: _____

Name _____ Date _____

ACTIVITY 81 REVIEWING ACCENT SKILLS

In the dictionary, a word may have a number of symbols that tell the sound, pronunciation, and accented syllables. In the exercise that follows, the words are listed with the phonetic spelling found in a dictionary. Complete the blanks for each word, and write a sentence using the word on the line provided.

Phonetic Spelling	Word	Syllable Division	Accented Syllable
1. klām	_____	_____	_____

Sentence: _____

| 2. kă fā′ | _____ | _____ | _____ |

Sentence: _____

| 3. měs′ən jər | _____ | _____ | _____ |

Sentence: _____

| 4. săl′ə rē | _____ | _____ | _____ |

Sentence: _____

| 5. păp′yo͞o lā′shən | _____ | _____ | _____ |

Sentence: _____

| 6. myo͞o nĭsh′ən | _____ | _____ | _____ |

Sentence: _____

| 7. bĭz′ē | _____ | _____ | _____ |

Sentence: _____

| 8. trŭb′əl | _____ | _____ | _____ |

Sentence: _____

| 9. kôt | _____ | _____ | _____ |

Sentence: _____

| 10. nĭt | _____ | _____ | _____ |

Sentence: _____

| 11. əb zʉrv′ə tôr′ē | _____ | _____ | _____ |

Sentence: _____

| 12. prō pôr′shən | _____ | _____ | _____ |

Sentence: _____

Name _____ Date _____

ACTIVITY 81 REVIEWING ACCENT SKILLS (CONTINUED)

Read each of the following sentences. Divide each highlighted word into syllables. Write the word on the blank with the accent mark correctly placed. Then, indicate the part of speech of the highlighted word. Use a dictionary, if necessary.

13. The **record** will speak for itself.

Syllables/Accent: _____ Part of Speech: _____

14. You have been chosen to **record** the results.

Syllables/Accent: _____ Part of Speech: _____

15. The **address** must be correctly written on the envelope.

Syllables/Accent: _____ Part of Speech: _____

16. When you **address** the class, you should speak clearly.

Syllables/Accent: _____ Part of Speech: _____

17. The coach will **permit** the team to play five games.

Syllables/Accent: _____ Part of Speech: _____

18. The **permit** you have is no longer valid for you to drive.

Syllables/Accent: _____ Part of Speech: _____

19. If you **refuse** to play, it will hurt the team's chance to win.

Syllables/Accent: _____ Part of Speech: _____

20. The **refuse** must be placed in the containers.

Syllables/Accent: _____ Part of Speech: _____

Name _____ Date _____

ACTIVITY 82	PHONICS REVIEW

For each of the words listed below, a description has been written for you to fill in. Read each description, fill in the blanks, and write the correct word on the blank below the description. You may use the dictionary.

delay   **tiger**   **exert**   **sable**   **robin**

1. This word has the spelling pattern VCV. There is an open and a closed syllable. One of the letters has the hard sound for "g." One syllable has a vowel followed by "r."
   a) The phonetic spelling is _____ .
   b) The first syllable is (open/closed).
   c) The vowel sound in the first syllable has a (macron/breve) above it because the sound is (long/short).
   d) The second syllable is (open/closed), and the vowel sound is controlled by the letter _____ .
   e) The vowel sound is shown with the (macron/schwa/breve).
   f) The accent is on the (first/second) syllable.
   g) The guide words on the page in the dictionary where the word is found are
      _____ and _____ .
   h) The word is _____ .

2. This word has the pattern VCCV and has two syllables. The second syllable has a silent "e." If the consonants "t," "c," or "l" were substituted for the beginning consonant in the first syllable, the sound of the second syllable would not change.
   a) The first syllable is (open/closed).
   b) The vowel sound of the first syllable is (long/short).
   c) The vowel sound in the first syllable is marked with the symbol (breve/macron/ schwa).
   d) The vowel sound for the second syllable is marked with the (breve/macron/schwa).
   e) The accent is on the (first/second) syllable.
   f) The guide words on the page in the dictionary where the word is found are
      _____ and _____ .
   g) The phonetic spelling for the word is _____ .
   h) The word is _____ .

Name _____ Date _____

ACTIVITY 82 PHONICS REVIEW (CONTINUED)

3. This word has the VCV pattern. There are two syllables, but the division is after the consonant in the first syllable. When this consonant is in a word, it usually stays in the syllable with the first vowel.
   a) The vowel sound of the first syllable is (long/short).
   b) The vowel sound in the second syllable is controlled by the letter____.
   c) The accent is on the (first/second) syllable.
   d) The guide words on the page in the dictionary where this word is found are

   _____ and _____ .
   e) The phonetic spelling for the word is _____ .
   f) The word is _____ .

4. This word has the VCV pattern. There are two syllables. When the syllable division of this word is after the first vowel, the word is a nonsense word. To correctly pronounce the word, give the first vowel the short sound. The syllable division is after the consonant that follows the first vowel.
   a) The accent of the word is on the (first/second) syllable.
   b) The vowel symbol of the first syllable is the (breve/macron/other).
   c) The vowel symbol of the second syllable is the (breve/macron/schwa).
   d) The guide words on the page where the word is found in the dictionary are

   _____ and _____ .
   e) The phonetic spelling for the word is _____ .
   f) The word is _____ .

5. This word has the VCV pattern. There is an open and a closed syllable. The second syllable ends in a letter that is silent. When this letter begins a word, it is a consonant. When it is at the end or middle of a word, it is a vowel.
   a) The first syllable is (open/closed).
   b) The vowel sound in the first syllable has a (macron/breve/schwa) symbol.
   c) The vowel in the second syllable is shown with the (macron/breve/schwa) symbol and has the (long/short) sound.
   d) The accent is on the (first/second) syllable.
   e) The guide words on the page where the word is found in the dictionary are

   _____ and _____ .
   f) The phonetic spelling of the word is _____ .
   g) The word is _____ .

Answer Keys

Activity 1 (page 10)

Group One	Group Two
1. ago	1. agent
2. boon	2. aghast
3. creed	3. algae
4. dead	4. algebra
5. deed	5. code
6. fan	6. color
7. flood	7. dorsal
8. giant	8. found
9. heavy	9. germ
10. jelly	10. good
11. king	11. grill
12. land	12. grit
13. magic	13. gutter
14. nudge	14. juice
15. orange	15. magic
16. peach	16. magnet
17. punt	17. number
18. range	18. orange
19. red	19. original
20. sale	20. quart
21. table	21. range
22. vegetable	22. stage
23. vertical	23. stake
24. wager	24. stale
25. yellow	25. stole

Activity 2 (page 11)

1. cope, cord, copper, cordial, coral, cooper, copy, copra
2. rectify, reform
3. rectify, recur, red, redeemer, redouble, reduce, reed, reflect, reflex, reform

Activity 3 (page 12)

Phonetic spellings may vary slightly depending on the dictionary used. Accept reasonable answers.
1b. to correct
  c. verb
2b. able to read and write
  c. adjective
3b. to happen or occur again
  c. verb
4b. to remove from office by the process of recall
  c. verb
5b. a written acknowledgement that something has been received
  c. noun
6b. in or on the inside; internally
  c. adverb
7b. any series of things in close or uninterrupted succession
  c. noun
8b. something done or given as a token or act of respect
  c. noun

Activity 4 (page 13)

Answers will vary according to the dictionary used.

Activity 5 (page 14)

1. feet	8. decide	15. passionate
2. festival	9. recess	16. wallop
3. mine	10. mutiny	17. textile
4. button	11. dollar	18. candy
5. cable	12. chemical	19. basket
6. haste	13. confess	20. riot
7. equal	14. nominate	

Activity 6 (page 15)

1. sphere, 2. arcing, 3. knew, 4. clear, 5. sphere, 6. defensive, 7. field, 8. sphere, 9. opportune, 10. glanced, 11. opponent, 12. sphere, 13. arc, 14. knew, 15. opponent, 16. impact, 17. sphere, 18. crossbar, 19. score, 20. point, 21. thrust, 22. force, 23. elated, 24. projected, 25. parabolic, 26. arc, 27. territory, 28. foot, 29. imminent, 30. collision, 31. incur, 32. prone, 33. ground, 34. engaged, 35. tête-à-tête, 36. dejected, 37. adversary, 38. team, 39. crucial, 40. goal

Activity 7 (page 16)

Initial Consonants	Final Consonants
b: bus, bird, box	d: nod, need, bird, bed
f: fox, fail	f: puff
j: jump	k: tack, milk, disk
l: lemon, last, ladder, listen	l: till, nail, dull
	m: slam
m: match, milk, must	n: lemon, robin, down
n: not, nine, needle, nap	p: jump, nap, mop
r: robin, rabbit, roar	r: car, ladder
t: tack, till, test	s: bus, mass
d: dust, down, disk, dull	t: last, dust, rabbit, mat
p: puff	z: fuzz, buzz

Activity 8 (page 17)

2. to, 3. so, 4. no
6. rake, 7. take, 8. fake, 9. lake, 10. bake
12. coy, 13. toy, 14. soy
16. lope, 17. mope, 18. rope, 19. dope, 20. cope

Activity 9 (page 17)

1. fast, 2. past, 3. cast, 4. mast, 5. last
6. fast, 7. cast, 8. mast, 9. last, 10. past
11. C, 12. E, 13. A, 14. B, 15. D

Activity 10 (page 18)
1. bade, 2. made, 3. fade, 4. jade, 5. wade
6. blade, 7. grade, 8. shade
9. tack, 10. lack, 11. mack, 12. pack, 13. rack, 14. sack
15–24. Words can be in any order. Teacher check sentences.
15. arcade, 17. blockade, 19. evade, 21. parade, 23. tirade
25–36. Similar rime words may be in any order. Teacher check sentences.
25. bound, 27. rebound, 29. surround, 31. divide, 33. pride, 35. reform

Activity 11 (page 19)
1. mash, 2. cash, 3. lash
4. list, 5. fist, 6. mist
7. last, 8. fast, 9. mist, 10. mast, 11. cast, 12. past, 13. fist, 14. list, 15. cash
16–22. Teacher check

Activity 12 (page 20)
1. Mack, 2. back, 3. sack, 4. tack, 5. lack, 6. rack
7. C, 8. D, 9. A, 10. E, 11. B
12. pack, 13. rack, 14. back, 15. sack
16–20. Teacher check

Activity 13 (page 21)
1. flock, 2. smock, 3. stock, 4. bedrock, 5. shamrock
6. encore, 7. lore, 8. carnivore, 9. herbivore, 10. adore
11. shade, 12. lemonade, 13. stockade, 14. spade, 15. jade

Activity 14 (page 22)
1. ō; 1; long; open; CV
2. ō; 1; long; open; CV
3. ē; 1; long; open; CV
4. ē; 1; long; open; CV
5. ē; 1; long; open; CV
6. ō; 1; long; open; CV
7. one, 8. one, 9. open, 10. CV

Activity 15 (pages 22–23)
1. ŏ; 1; short; closed; CVC
2. ŏ; 1; short; closed; CVC
3. ĕ; 1; short; closed; CVC
4. ĕ; 1; short; closed; CVC
5. ĕ; 1; short; closed; CVC
6. ŏ; 1; short; closed; CVC
7. one, 8. one, 9. closed, 10. CVC

Activity 16 (page 23)
3. kit; i; short; CVC; kĭt
4. kite; i, e; long; CVCV; kīte̸

5. hat; a; short; CVC; hăt
6. hate; a, e; long; CVCV; hāte̸
7. tub; u; short; CVC; tŭb
8. tube; u, e; long; CVCV; tūbe̸
9. dot; o; short; CVC; dŏt
10. dote; o, e; long; CVCV; dōte̸
11. met; e; short; CVC; mĕt
12. mete; e, e; long; CVCV; mēte̸
13. ban; a; short; CVC; băn
14. bane; a, e; long; CVCV; bāne̸
15. lob; o; short; CVC; lŏb
16. lobe; o, e; long; CVCV; lōbe̸
17. bar; a; short; CVC; băr
18. bare; a, e; long; CVCV; bāre̸
19. gal; a; short; CVC; găl
20. gale; a, e; long; CVCV; gāle̸

Activity 17 (page 24)
1. a; short; CVC; făn
2. e; short; CVC; lĕd
3. i, e; long; CVCV; rīce̸
4. a, e; long; CVCV; fāme̸
5. e; short; CVC; lĕt
6. i; short; CVC; mĭt
7. i; short; CVC; hĭm
8. u, e; long; CVCV; cūte̸
9. u; short; CVC; bŭn
10. i; short; CVC; pĭn
11. i, e; long; CVCV; vīne̸
12. o, e; long; CVCV; dōme̸
13. o; short; CVC; cŏt
14. i, e; long; CVCV; rīme̸
15. a, e; long; CVCV; cāne̸
16. u; short; CVC; sŭn
17. i; short CVC; lĭp
18. u, e; long; CVCV; lūte̸
19. i, e; long; CVCV; līme̸
20. a, e; long; CVCV; lāke̸
21. a; short; CVC; răn
22. e; short; CVC; sĕt
23. o; short; CVC; fŏx
24. i, e; long; CVCV; tīde̸
25. u, e; long; CVCV dūde̸

Activity 18 (page 25)
1. stāge̸
2. chīde̸
3. scrībe̸
4. jūte̸
5. drōne̸
6. prūne̸
7. grīme̸
8. fūme̸
9. smōte̸
10. mīme̸
11. drāpe̸
12. vāne̸

Activity 19 (page 26)

1. a, e; long; e	12. a, e; long; e
2. a; short	13. a; short
3. o, e; long; e	14. a; short
4. o, e; long; e	15. o; short
5. e; short	16. a, e; long; e
6. i; short	17. e; short
7. o; long	18. u; short
8. o; short	19. o; short
9. e; short	20. i; short
10. i, e; long; e	21. e; short
11. u; short	22. i; short

Activity 20 (page 27)

1. long "e"
2. short "e"
3. long "e"
4. short "e"
5. short "e"
6–10. Teacher check sentences
11. ⁻ 12. ⁻ 13. ⁻ 14. ˘ 15. ˘
16. dĕad, 17. sprĕad, 18. strēam

Activity 21 (page 28)

1. long "i"
2. long "i"
3. long "e"
4. long "e"
5. long "i"
6—10. Teacher check sentences
11. i   12. i   13. e   14. e   15. i

16. achi͟eve, 17. fri͟ed, 18. bri͟ef

Activity 22 (page 29)

1. long "e"	5. long "e"
2. long "a"	6. long "e"
3. long "a"	7. long "a"
4. long "e"	8. long "e"

9—13. Teacher check sentences

14. we͟ight, 15. fre͟ight, 16. rece͟ipt, 17. perce͟ive

18. re͟ign

Activity 23 (page 30)

1. Pool: cool, fool, drool, loose, school, goose
2. Took: book, hood, hoof, stood

3. pool	7. pool
4. pool	8. took
5. took	9. pool
6. took	10. took

11—18. Teacher check sentences

Activity 24 (page 31)

1. Know: snow, show, pillow, sparrow
2. Cow: power, shower, crowd, growl, clown, renowned, scow, howl, town, bow, plowed, brown, howitzer
3. coward
4. tower
5. cowboy, frown, towered, clown
6. brow, towel, blow
7. flowers, grow, below, snow
8. brown, glowered
9. know, shadow, snow, grow
10. frown, brow, flowers

Activity 25 (page 32)

field: achieved, chief, relief, hygiene, shield
die: tried, pie, dried, fried
seat: team, beach, stream, cream, eat, beans, each
either: leisure
free: need, beef
took: good, book, look
cool: school, smooth, blooming
cow: down, flowers

Activity 26 (page 33)

1—5. Words may be in any order.
1. blink, 2. shrink, 3. slink, 4. clink, 5. drink

6. st	7. squ	8. sch	9. scr	10. sl
11. pr	12. pl	13. dr	14. gr	15. br
16. sw	17. cl	18. tr	19. spl	20. fr

Teacher check sentences

Activity 27 (page 34)

1. ft	2. nd	3. nt	4. ft	5. st
6. sp	7. ng	8. pt	9. nk	10. ng
11. nd	12. st	13. sp	14. nt	15. pt
16. lk	17. ft	18. nk	29. ng	20. nt

Teacher check sentences

Activity 28 (pages 35–36)

1a. fling, b. sang, c. stung, d. song
e—h. Teacher check sentences
i. i, a, u, o
j. short
k. one
l. one
m. one
n. closed
2a. kept, b. crept, c. slept, d. prompt
e—h. Teacher check sentences
i. e, e, e, o
j. short
k. one
l. one

m. one
n. closed
3a. tank, b. spank, c. blink, d. drunk
   e—h. Teacher check sentences
   i. a, a, i, u
   j. short
   k. one
   l. one
   m. one
   n. closed
4a. spend, b. band, c. pond, d. lend
   e—h. Teacher check sentences
   i. e, a, o, e
   j. short
   k. two
   l. one
   m. one
   n. closed
5a. left, b. drift, c. craft, d. deft
   e—h. Teacher check sentences
   i. e, i, a, e
   j. short
   k. one
   l. one
   m. one
   n. closed

Activity 29 (page 37)
Climate, plants, grow, prairie, plants, scrawny, flowers, splendid, fruit, plants, struggle, stressful, climate, grouse, strut, flourish, climate, stressful, dromedary, plod, frigate, glare, driver, blizzard, cruel, flamingo, blizzard, gratifying, bliss

Activity 30 (pages 37—38)
1. br	2. dr	3. st	4. bl	5. sm	6. pl
7. scr	8. sl	9. pr	10. sw	11. pr	12. sch
13. cl	14. str	15. sch	16. gr	17. spr	18. sp
19. fr	20. str	21. tr	22. tr	23. br	24. br
25. sw	26. tr	27. pr	28. sh	29. br	

Activity 31 (page 38)
1. cl	2. tr	3. bl
4. sp	5. sm	6. cr
7. sl	8. pl	9. scr
10. qu	11. pl	12. mp
13. lf	14. sk	15. gr

16. end, middle
17. true
18. false; Blends are not found only at the beginning of a word.
19. false; Blends can consist of two or three consonants.
20. false; Blends that are found at the end of a word can also be used at the beginning of a word.

Activity 32 (pages 39—40)
Teacher check sentences and (c) answers
1a. chin, b. chair
2a. shin, b. sharp
3a. phase, b. phony
4a. their, b. then
5a. what, b. whale
6. ch	7. th	8. wh	9. wh	10. ch
11. gh	12. th	13. sh	14. ph	15. ph
16. th	17. gh	18. sh	19. ch	20. wh

Activity 33 (page 41)
1. church	7. chef
2. church	8. school
3. church	9. school
4. chef	10. church
5. chef	11. school
6. church	

Activity 34 (page 42)
ch, th, ph, wh, th, ph, sh, ch, ch, th, th, th, th, th, ch, ph, th, sh, th, wh, wh, wh, sh, sh, sh, th, th, th, ch, th, th, sh, ch, wh, th, th, th, th, th, th, ch, th, ch, th, th, th, sh, wh

Activity 35 (pages 43—44)
Words may be in any order within each group. Teacher check sentences.
1a. dispatch, b. grouch, c. hatch, d. batch
2a. smack, b. frock, c. brick, d. slack
3a. bath, b. smooth, c. cloth, d. smith
4a. rash, b. smash, c. squish, d. thresh
5a. laugh, b. cough, c. tough, d. slough
6a. swing, b. fling, c. song. d. clang
7a. dodge, b. grudge, c. smudge, d. ledge
8. sh	9. gh	10. ch	11. th	12. ng
13. gh	14. dge	15. ck		

Activity 36 (page 45)
1a. sh	b. ck	c. gh	d. ch
e. ph	f. ph	g. ph	h. ch
i. kn	j. ph	k. th	l. th
m. ck			

2. end, middle
3. false; In digraphs, the letters combine to make a new sound.
4. false; Digraphs are found at the beginning, end, or in the middle of a word.
5—10. Teacher check sentences. Some words may vary. Possible answers are given.
5. clink
6. ledge, dredge, hedge
7. detach
8. able, cable, table
9. than
10. thank

Activity 37 (pages 46–47)

1. k, hard	6. c, soft
2. c, soft	7. k, hard
3. k, hard	8. c, soft
4. k, hard	9. c, soft
5. c, soft	10. c, soft

11–14. camp, card, cart, cube (Teacher check sentences)
15–20. Answers will vary.
21. Hard: Cal, call, collie, calmly, Callie, cat, cage, colored, casual, could, careless, caress, caught, cautiously, collar, cake, cool
22. Soft: ceiling, Cindy, center, cinnamon, circus, center, cedar

Activity 38 (pages 48–49)

1. j, soft	6. j, soft
2. j, soft	7. j, soft
3. g, hard	8. g, hard
4. g, hard	9. g, hard
5. g, hard	10. j, soft

11–14. germ, gentle, genie, gem (Teacher check sentences)
15–18. gold, glass, good, green (Teacher check sentences)
19. Hard: glass, gold, green, gallin, game, glad, goose, program
20. Soft: George, orange, cabbage, large, judges

Activity 39 (page 50)

1. Hard "g": gab, gave, gallon, gate
2. Soft "g": gyp, gem, gently, giant, ginger, geography, gypsy, general, germ
3. Hard "c": came, canoe, capital, calm, candy, camp, cane, canyon
4. Soft "c": cycle, cell, cent, city, cider, certain, cyclone, center

Activity 40 (page 51)

1. sox (ks): box, fox, toxic
2. exit (gz): extension, exert, explain
3. xerox (z): xylem, xenon, xebec, xylophone
4. ex/ert, gz
5. ex/am, gz
6. ex/alt, gz
7. ex/empt, gz
8. ex/ist, gz
9. ex/ude, gz
10. ex/e/cute, ks

Activity 41 (pages 52–53)

Teacher check sentences
1a. one; b. closed; c. short; d. digraph; e. /kw/
2a. one; b. closed; c. short; d. digraph; e. /kw/
3a. one; b. closed; c. a; d. long; e. silent; f. /kw/

4a. one; b. closed; c. o; d. long; silent; f. /kw/
5a. two; b. open; c. e; d. short; e. sounded; f. /kw/
6a. two; b. open; c. r; d. /kw/
7a. two; b. short; c. silent; d. /k/

Activity 42 (page 54)

All blanks are "kw" except for 19, 20, and 21, which are "k."

Activity 43 (page 55)

Teacher check sentences
1. nash; a. closed; b. short; c. digraph; d. form a new sound
2. nu; a. open; b. long
3. narl; a. closed; b. r-controlled
4. nom; a. closed; b. long; c. g, e
5. nostic; a. two; b. closed; c. short; d. short; e. s, t

Activity 44 (page 56)

Teacher check sentences
1. nif; a. closed; b. i; c. long; d. k, e
2. ned; a. closed; b. e; c. long; d. k, a
3. nukel; a. two; b. u; c. short; d. k, c
4. ne; a. open; b. e; c. long; d. k, e
5. napsak; a. closed; b. a; c. short; d. k, c

Activity 45 (page 57)

Teacher check sentences
1. cam; a. one; b. closed; c. a; d. short; e. l
2. woud; a. closed; c. o, u; d. l
3. wak; a. one; b. closed; c. a; d. l
4. chak; a. one; b. closed; c. a; d. l

Activity 46 (page 58)

Teacher check sentences
1. hi; a. g, h; b. i; c. open; d. long
2. fiter; a. g, h; b. i, e; c. e; d. open; e. long
3. taut; a. g, h; b. a, u; c. caught
4. sit; a. g, h; b. i; c. long; d. closed

Activity 47 (page 59)

Teacher check sentences
1. lisen; a. two; b. closed; c. i, e; d. short; e. schwa; f. t
2. ofen; a. two; b. closed; c. o, e; d. short; e. schwa; f. t
3. thisel; a. two; b. s, t; c. closed; d. i, e; e. short; f. t
4. casel; a. two; b. s, t; c. closed; d. a, e; e. short; f. t

Activity 48 (page 60)

Teacher check sentences
1. rit; a. one; b. closed; c. i, e; d. long; e. w, e
2. rist; a. one; b. closed; c. i, d, short; e. w. f. blend
3. rapper; a. two; b. closed; c. a, e; d. short; e. w
4. rekage; a. two; b. closed; c. age; d. short; w, c, e

Activity 49 (page 61)
1. g   2. b   3. b   4. e   5. e
6. n   7. w   8. t   9. gh   10. l
11–25. Teacher check. Phonetic spellings may vary according to the dictionary used.

Activity 50 (page 62)

1.	1	1	1	9.	2	1	1
2.	2	1	1	10.	2	1	1
3.	2	2	2	11.	3	2	2
4.	2	1	1	12.	2	2	2
5.	2	1	1	13.	4	4	4
6.	3	2	2	14.	3	3	3
7.	4	2	2	15.	4	3	3
8.	3	1	1				

Activity 51 (page 63)
Teacher check sentences
2. VCCV, rab/bit, rab, short, bit, short
3. VCCV, pen/cil, pen, short, cil, other
4. VCCV, cir/cus, cir, other, cus, short
5. VCCV, prob/lem, prob, short, lem, short
6. VCCV, par/don, par, other, don, short
7. VCCV, gob/let, gob, short, let, short
8. VCCV, plas/tic, plas, short, tic, short
9. VCCV, cor/ner, cor, other, ner, other
10. VCCV, bur/den, bur, other, den, short

Activity 52 (page 64)
1. circus, after, dinner, Molly, sister, also, cellar, getting, ladder, mother, picture, helping, carpet

2.

Word	Spelling Pattern	Syllable Division
circus	VCCV	cir/cus
after	VCCV	af/ter
dinner	VCCV	din/ner
Molly	VCCV	Mol/ly
sister	VCCV	sis/ter
also	VCCV	al/so
cellar	VCCV	cel/lar
getting	VCCV	get/ting
ladder	VCCV	lad/der
mother	VCCV	moth/er
picture	VCCV	pic/ture
helping	VCCV	hel/ping
carpet	VCCV	car/pet

Activity 53 (page 65)
2. ph, hy/phen
3. ph, neph/ew
4. ng, sing/er
5. sh, cash/ier
6. gh, laugh/a/ble
7. th, lath/er
8. ch, pur/chase

9. th, fa/ther
10. gh, tough/est

Activity 54 (page 66)
Teacher check sentences
2. VCV, ti/ger, ti, long, ger, other
3. VCV, pa/per, pa, long, per, other
4. VCV, to/tem, to, long, tem, short
5. VCV, fa/tal, fa, long, tal, other
6. VCV, pi/lot, pi, long, lot, short
7. VCV, i/tem, i, long, tem, short
8. VCV, ve/to, ve, long, to, long
9. VCV, tu/lip, tu, long, lip, short
10. VCV, pu/pil, pu, long, pil, other

Activity 55 (page 67)
VCCV: basket, butter, garden, dollars, often, only
VCV: paper, tulip, bacon, lemon, vacant, fine, vital, total, time, cedar, today, silent, halo, open, petals, music
1–8. Teacher check

Activity 56 (page 68)
Teacher check sentences
2. Cle, pur/ple, pur, other, ple, other
3. Cle, ta/ble, ta, long, ble, other
4. Cle, stum/ble, stum, short, ble, other
5. Cle, sam/ple, sam, short, ple, other
6. Cle, sin/gle, sin, short, gle, other
7. Cle, mar/ble, mar, other, ble, other
8. Cle, fum/ble, fum, short, ble, other
9. Cle, tan/gle, tan, short, gle, other
10. Cle, sta/ple, sta, long, ple, other

Activity 57 (page 69)
VCCV: sur/face, pen/cil, bas/ket, sil/ver, mir/ror, dance, skipped
VCV: lake, pa/per, to/day, a/way, wa/ter
Cle: ta/ble, peb/ble, cir/cles, un/cle, an/gle, sin/gle
Other: hit, rock, did

Activity 58 (page 70)

Root Word	Affixes
1. help	-ful; -ing; -ed
2. light	re-; -ed; re-, -ed
3. sure	un-; -ly; in-
4. trust	dis-; dis-, -ing; en-
5. capture	re-; -ing; -ed
6. match	-ed; mis-; re-
7. check	-ed; re-, -ing; -ing
8. fast	-er; -ing; -est
9. light	de-; de-, -ful; de-, -ed
10. place	mis-; mis-, -ed; re-
11. please	-d, dis-, -ing
12. late	-er; -ly; -est
13. note	de-; -able; -ed

14. park   -s; -ing; -ed
15. close   en-; dis-; -ed
16. nation   -al; -s; inter-, -al
17. desire   -ed; -able; -ing
18. step   mis-; -ing; -ed
19. love   -able; -ly; -ing
20. pay   re-; -ment; -able

Activity 59 (page 71)
1. boy, s (plural)
2. boy, 's (possession)
3. baby, 's, (possession)
4. men, 's (possession)
5. sing, ing (tense change)
6. tall, est (degree change)
7. brush, es (plural)
8. lamp, s (plural)
9. play, ed (tense change)
10. calm, er (degree change)
11–15. Teacher check
16–20. Students may add either "er" or "est" to form the comparative or superlative adjective.
16. quicker/quickest; er/est; quickly; ly
17. shorter/shortest; er/est; shortly; ly
18. slower/slowest; er/est; slowly; ly
19. quieter/quietest; er/est; quietly; ly
20. swifter/swiftest; er/est; swiftly; ly

Activity 60 (pages 72–73)
Teacher check sentences
1. less, Changes part of speech
2. est, Makes meaning clearer
3. ly, Changes part of speech
4. est, Makes meaning clearer
5. ful, Changes part of speech
6. ify, Changes part of speech
7. ive, Changes part of speech
8. ful, Changes part of speech
9. less, Changes part of speech
10. ish, Changes part of speech
11. ly, Changes part of speech
12. ity, Changes part of speech
13. ion, Changes part of speech
14. able, Changes part of speech
15. ism, Changes part of speech

Activity 61 (page 74)
Some words may be matched with more than one prefix. All possible answers are given. Teacher check sentences.
1. rainy   6. sadly, sadder
2. homely/homeless   7. foolish
3. dependable   8. excitement/exciteable
4. careful/careless   9. heroic
5. worker/workable   10. selfish/selfless

Activity 62 (page 75)
1. Drop the "y" and add an "i" before the suffix.
2. Drop the "y" and add an "i" before the suffix.
3. Drop the "y" and add an "i" before the suffix.
4. Drop the "y" and add an "i" before the suffix.
5. Drop the "y" and add an "i" before the suffix.
6. y; 7. consonant; 8. y
9a. y; b. consonant; c. y; d. i
Some of the following words may be matched with more than one suffix. All possible answers are given.
10. tiniest   16. capped/capping
11. cheeriest/cheeriness   17. stopped/stopping
12. multiplied   18. batted/batting
13. beautiful   19. dropped/dropping
14. happiest/happiness   20. stabbed/stabbing

Activity 63 (page 76)
5. y   6. vowel   7a. y; b. vowel
8. saying
9–11. All possible answers are given.
9. deployed/deploying/deployment
10. enjoyed/enjoying/enjoyment
11. strayed/straying
12. y   13. consonant
14. y   15. no   16. i
17. hurrying   18. flying   19. trying
20a. i; b. is not; c. suffix

Activity 64 (page 77)
1. C   2. A   3. B   4. E   5. F   6. D
7. e   8. vowel   9. e
10a. e; b. vowel; c. e
11. enjoy   12. girl
13. smile   14. desire
15. excite   16. complete
17. skinny   18. atmosphere
19. wonder   20. botany

Activity 65 (pages 78–79)
Teacher check sentences
1. wickedness (noun); wicked (adjective)
2. attraction (noun); attract (verb)
3. expensive (adjective); expense (noun)
4. loyalist (noun); loyal (adjective)
5. lovable (adjective); love (noun/verb)
6. creamery (noun); cream (noun/verb)
7. difference (noun); differ (verb)
8. penniless (adjective); penny (noun)
9. commercial (adjective); commerce (noun)
10. stationary (adjective); station (noun)
11. enclosure (noun); enclose (verb)
12. prosperous (adjective); prosper (verb)
13. allowance (noun); allow (verb)
14. historic (adjective); history (noun)
15. narration (noun); narrate (verb)

Activity 66 (page 80)
1. nation, 2. basic, 3. commit, 4. money, 5. obligate, 6. protect, 7. educate, 8. enforce, 9. distribute, 10. employ, 11. prosper, 12. addition, 13. tax, 14. commerce, 15. resident

16. B   17. D   18. A   19. D   20. C
21. C   22. C   23. A   24. C   25. A
26. D   27. B   28. C   29. B   30. B

Activity 67 (page 81)
Teacher check sentences
1. happy; un   2. part; de   3. call; re
4. agree; dis   5. even; un   6. order; dis
7. close; en   8. pair; re   9. certain; un
10. large; en   11. print; im   12. take; in
13. stop; non

Activity 68 (page 82)
Teacher check sentences
1. dis   2. im   3. mis   4. re
5. re   6. un   7. in   8. dis

Activity 69 (page 83)
1. impolite   not polite
2. indecent   not decent
3. insecure   not secure
4. impure   not pure
5. misspell   spell wrong
6. unfair   not fair
7. misunderstand   understand wrong
8. irregular   not regular
9. overreact   react too strongly
10. import   bring in
11. incapable   not capable
12. discontinue   not continue
13. dissatisfied   not satisfied
14. uncivilized   not civilized
15. irrational   not rational
16. illegal   not legal
17. misapply   apply wrong
18. inappropriate   not appropriate
19. reapply   apply again
20. repay   pay again

Activity 70 (page 84)
1. de   2. mis   3. en   4. inter   5. un
6. im   7. dis   8. in   9. re   10. non
11–20. Teacher check sentences

Activity 71 (page 85)
Teacher check paragraph.
1. scheduled, 2. satisfied, 3. rational, 4. relevant, 5. correct, 6. applying, 7. probable, 8. test, 9. material
10. dis   11. im   12. mis   13. in   14. in   15. un
16. dis   17. dis   18. in   19. mis   20. re

Activity 72 (page 86)
Teacher check phonetic spellings. They may vary slightly according to the dictionary used.
2. active; in/ac/tive
3. happy; un/hap/py
4. paid; re/paid
5. press; im/press
6. large; en/large
7. sensitive; in/sen/si/tive
8. comfort; dis/com/fort
9. twist; un/twist
10. septic; an/ti/sep/tic
11. muscular; in/tra/mus/cu/lar
12. climax; an/ti/cli/max
13. stabilize; de/sta/bi/lize
14. consistent; in/con/sis/tent
15. divide; sub/di/vide

Activity 73 (page 87)
Teacher check phonetic spellings. They may vary slightly according to the dictionary used.
1. pay; re; ment   11. polite
2. success; un; ful   12. fresh
3. built; re   13. operate; co; ive
4. conduct; non; or   14. judge; ment
5. meaning; less   15. literate; il
6. destruct; ive   16. found; un; ed
7. apply; mis; cation   17. tract; re
8. mort; im; al   18. take; mis; en
9. direct   19. globe; al
10. history; pre; ic   20. wrist

Activity 74 (page 88)
Teacher check sentences
1. unnaturally   6. recaptured
2. semicircular   7. impersonal
3. hemispherical   8. biodiversity
4. disrespectful   9. misdirection
5. international   10. unselfish

Activity 75 (page 89)
1. police   man   6. road; railroad
2. fire   place   7. car; streetcar
3. side   walk   8. bell; doorbell
4. work   shop   9. town; downtown
5. any   body   10. plane; airplane

11. C   12. A   13. D   14. E   15. B

Activity 76 (page 90)
Teacher check sentences and phonetic spellings.
1. down/wind; down; in the direction in which the wind is blowing
2. main/stream; main; the part of something considered to be the most active, productive, etc.

3. proof/read; proof; to read and mark correction on
4. land/mass; land; a very large area of land, especially a continent
5. out/lay; out; a spending (of money, energy, etc.)
6. afternoon, springtime, sunlight, into, bedroom, streetcar, downtown, birthday, downstairs, basketball, fireplace, basketball, outside, basketball, cardboard, football, baseball, streetcar

Activity 77 (page 91)
1. keynote; the basic idea or ruling principle
2. greenhorn; an inexperienced person
3. footnote; an additional comment
4. hardship; a difficult circumstance
5. whitewash; to cover up or conceal
6. doghouse; in trouble
7. fireworks; a noisy quarrel or display of anger
8. hardware; articles made of metal (in this case a trophy)
9. hamstring; to hamper or lessen the effectiveness of
10. highlight; to emphasize

Activity 78 (page 92)
1. ac/cept; 3; cept
2. com/plain; 2; plain
3. rea/son; 2; rea
4. a/ble; 2; a
5. po/lite; 2; lite
6. ho/ri/zon; 3; ri
7. ma/te/ri/al; 4; te
8. pet/ri/fy; 3; pet
9. sen/si/tive; 3; sen
10. en/ve/lope; 3; en

Activity 79 (pages 93–94)
Answers (a) and (b) may be in either order. Teacher check sentences.
1a. com/pound; com; noun
 b. com/pound; pound; verb
2a. ad/dress; ad; noun
 b. ad/dress; dress; verb
3a. trans/fer; trans; noun
 b. trans/fer; fer; verb
4a. per/mit; per; noun
 b. per/mit; mit; verb
5a. fre/quent; fre; adjective
 b. fre/quent; quent; verb
6a. ab/sent; ab; adjective
 b. ab/sent; sent; verb
7a. col/lect; col; noun
 b. col/lect; lect; verb/adjective/adverb
8a. con/tent; con; noun
 b. con/tent; tent; adjective
9a. di/gest; di; noun
 b. di/gest; gest; verb
10a. com/plex; com; noun
 b. com/plex; plex; adjective

Activity 80 (page 95)
1. tow/el; tow; el
2. be/lieve; lieve; be
3. sec/ond; sec; ond
4. del/ta; del/ ta
5. el/e/ment; el; e
Teacher check sentences and phonetic spellings. They may vary according to the dictionary used.
6. con/gru/i/ty; gru; con/ /i/ty
7. gen/try; gen; try
8. in/el/o/quent; el; en/ /o/quent
9. pro/duc/tion; duc; pro/ /tion
10. ul/cer/ate; ul; /cer/ate

Activity 81 (pages 96–97)
Teacher check sentences
1. claim; claim; claim
2. cafe; ca/fe; fe
3. messenger; mes/sen/ger; mes
4. salary; sal/a/ry; sal
5. population; pop/u/la/tion; la
6. munition; mu/ni/tion; ni
7. busy; bus/y; bus
8. trouble; trou/ble; trou
9. caught; caught; caught
10. knit; knit; knit
11. observatory; ob/serv/a/to/ry; serv
12. proportion; pro/por/tion; por
13. re'/cord; noun
14. re/cord'; verb
15. ad'/dress; noun
16. ad/dress'; verb
17. per/mit'; verb
18. per'/mit; noun
19. re/fuse'; verb
20. ref'/use; noun

Activity 82 (pages 98–99)
Dictionary guide words will vary according to the dictionary used.
1a. tī' gər; b. open; c. macron, long; d. closed, r; e. schwa; f. first; h. tiger
2a. open; b. long; c. macron; d. schwa; e. first; g. sā' bəl; h. sable
3a. short; b. r; c. second; e. ĕg zʉrt'; f. exert
4a. first; b. other; c. schwa; e. rä' bən; f. robin
5a. open; b. macron; c. macron, long; d. second; f. dē lā'; g. delay

108